Russell Library
Middletown, CT 06457

A 2140 545742 4

withdrawn

D1528870

J
398.2452
GOD

08/10

Children's Services
Russell Library
123 Broad Street
Middletown, CT 06457

withdrawn

MYSTERIES, LEGENDS, AND UNEXPLAINED PHENOMENA

MYTHICAL CREATURES

MYSTERIES, LEGENDS, AND UNEXPLAINED PHENOMENA

Contents

Foreword

Did you ever have an experience that turned your whole world upside down? Maybe you saw a ghost or a UFO. Perhaps you had an unusual, vivid dream that seemed real. Maybe you suddenly knew that a certain event was going to happen in the future. Or, perhaps you saw a creature or a being that did not fit the description of anything known in the natural world. At first you might have thought your imagination was playing tricks on you. Then, perhaps, you wondered about what you experienced and went looking for an explanation.

Every day and night people have experiences they can't explain. For many people these events are life changing. Their comfort zone of what they can accept as "real" is put to the test. It takes only one such experience for people to question the reality of the mysterious worlds that might exist beyond the one we live in. Perhaps you haven't encountered the unknown, but you have an intense curiosity about it. Either way, by picking up this book, you've started an adventure to explore and learn more, and you've come to the right place! The book you hold has been written by a leading expert in the paranormal—someone who understands unusual experiences and who knows the answers to your questions.

As a seeker of knowledge, you have plenty of company. Mythology, folklore, and records of the past show that human beings have had paranormal experiences throughout history. Even prehistoric cave paintings and gravesites indicate that early humans had concepts of the supernatural and of an afterlife. Humans have always sought to understand paranormal experiences and to put them into a frame of reference that makes sense to us in our daily lives. Some of the greatest minds in history have grappled with questions about the paranormal. For example, Greek philosopher Plato pondered the nature of dreams and how we "travel" during them. Isaac Newton was interested in the esoteric study of alchemy, which has magical elements, and St. Thomas Aquinas explored the nature of angels and spirits. Philosopher William James joined organizations dedicated to psychical research; and even the inventor of the light bulb, Thomas Alva Edison, wanted to build a device that could talk to the dead. More recently, physicists such as David Bohm, Stephen Hawking, William Tiller, and Michio Kaku have developed ideas that may help explain how and why paranormal phenomena happen, and neuroscience researchers like Michael Persinger have explored the nature of consciousness.

Exactly what is a paranormal experience or phenomenon? "Para" is derived from a Latin term for "beyond." So "paranormal" means "beyond normal," or things that do not fit what we experience through our five senses alone and which do not follow the laws we observe in nature and in science. Paranormal experiences and phenomena run the gamut from the awesome and marvelous, such as angels and miracles, to the downright terrifying, such as vampires and werewolves.

Paranormal experiences have been consistent throughout the ages, but explanations of them have changed as societies, cultures, and technologies have changed. For example, our ancestors were much closer to the invisible realms. In times when life was simpler, they saw, felt, and experienced other realities on a daily basis. When night fell, the darkness was thick and quiet, and it was easier to see unusual things, such as ghosts. They had no electricity to keep the night lit up. They had no media for constant communication and entertainment. Travel was difficult. They had more time to notice subtle things that were just beyond their ordinary senses. Few doubted their experiences. They accepted the invisible realms as an extension of ordinary life.

Today, we have many distractions. We are constantly busy, from the time we wake up until we go to bed. The world is full of light and noise 24 hours a day, seven days a week. We have television, the Internet, computer games, and cell phones to keep us busy, busy, busy.

We are ruled by technology and science. Yet, we still have paranormal experiences very similar to those of our ancestors. Because these occurrences do not fit neatly into science and technology, many people think they are illusions, and there are plenty of skeptics always ready to debunk the paranormal and reinforce that idea.

In roughly the past 100 years, though, some scientists have studied the paranormal and attempted to find scientific evidence for it. Psychic phenomena have proven difficult to observe and measure according to scientific standards. However, lack of scientific proof does not mean paranormal experiences do not happen. Courageous scientists are still looking for bridges between science and the supernatural.

My personal experiences are behind my lifelong study of the paranormal. Like many children I had invisible playmates when I was very young, and I saw strange lights in the yard and woods that I instinctively knew were the nature spirits who lived there. Children seem to be very open to paranormal phenomena, but their ability to have these experiences often fades away as they become more involved in the outside world, or, perhaps, as adults tell them not to believe in what they experience, that it's only in their imagination. Even when I was very young, I was puzzled that other people would tell me with great authority that I did not experience what I knew I did.

A major reason for my interest in the paranormal is precognitive dreaming experienced by members of my family. Precognition means "fore knowing," or knowing the future. My mother had a lot of psychic experiences, including dreams of future events. As a teen it seemed amazing to me that dreams could show us the future. I was determined to learn more about this and to have such dreams myself. I found books that explained extrasensory perception, the knowing of information beyond the five senses. I learned about dreams and experimented with them. I taught myself to visit distant places in my dreams and to notice details about them that I could later verify in the physical world. I learned how to send people telepathic messages in dreams and how to receive messages in dreams. Every night became an exciting adventure.

Those interests led me to other areas of the paranormal. Pretty soon I was engrossed in studying all kinds of topics. I learned different techniques for divination, including the Tarot. I learned how to meditate. I took courses to develop my own psychic skills, and I gave psychic readings to others. Everyone has at least some natural psychic ability and can improve it with attention and practice.

Next I turned my attention to the skies, to ufology, and what might be "out there" in space. I studied the lore of angels and fairies. I delved into the dark shadowy realm of demons and monsters. I learned the principles of real magic and spell casting. I undertook investigations of haunted places. I learned how to see auras and do energy healing. I even participated in some formal scientific laboratory experiments for telepathy.

My studies led me to have many kinds of experiences that have enriched my understanding of the paranormal. I cannot say that I can prove anything in scientific terms. It may be some time yet before science and the paranormal stop flirting with each other and really get together. Meanwhile, we can still learn a great deal from our personal experiences. At the very least, our paranormal experiences contribute to our inner wisdom. I encourage others to do the same as I do. Look first for natural explanations of strange phenomena. If natural explanations cannot be found or seem unlikely, consider paranormal explanations. Many paranormal experiences fall into a vague area, where although natural causes might exist, we simply don't know what could explain them. In that case I tell people to trust their intuition that they had a paranormal experience. Sometimes the explanation makes itself known later on.

I have concluded from my studies and experiences that invisible dimensions are layered upon our world, and that many paranormal experiences occur when there are openings between worlds. The doorways often open at unexpected times. You take a trip, visit a haunted place, or have a strange dream—and suddenly reality shifts. You get a glimpse behind the curtain that separates the ordinary from the extraordinary.

The books in this series will introduce you to these exciting and mysterious subjects. You'll learn many things that will astonish you. You'll be given lots of tips for how to explore the paranormal on your own. Paranormal investigation is a popular field, and you don't have to be a scientist or a full-time researcher to explore it. There are many things you can do in your free time. The knowledge you gain from these books will help prepare you for any unusual and unexpected experiences.

As you go deeper into your study of the paranormal, you may come up with new ideas for explanations. That's one of the appealing aspects of paranormal investigation—there is always room for bold ideas. So, keep an open and curious mind, and think big. Mysterious worlds are waiting for you!

—Rosemary Ellen Guiley

Introduction

Winged horses, one-eyed giants, and monstrous, intelligent lizards with fire in their breath—these impossible creatures romp through the ancient storehouse of myth and legend that is humanity's shared legacy. People have always wondered two things: Where did the idea of mythic beasts originate, and is it possible they still exist *outside* the written page or whispered tale?

The questions do not stop there. It is tempting to ask whether the Egyptians modeled their eerie, half human and half lion **Sphinx** on some beast glimpsed by priests who could see visitors from other worlds. Could ancient accounts of "gods" be based on actual creatures, living or extinct? Many historians believe dragons are "almost certainly" derived from sightings of giant snakes such as boa constrictors.[1] And dinosaur bones may have inspired thoughts of other monsters in the imagination of early man.

When looking at ancient mythology, it may help to remember that these tales involve much more than simple descriptions of weird creatures. The great myths of civilization are not just collections of fairy tales or children's stories. They are meant to carry the great teachings of society to each generation through the power of vivid imagery. And what image could be more powerful than a creature that is not only monstrous in size, but is made of parts of many different beasts with special characteristics and powers?

"The mythology of India could be said to describe every experience and emotion of man," notes *Indian Mythology* by Veronica Ions.[2] The Hindu character **Garuda**, for example, is part human, part eagle. Known as the king of all birds, Garuda possesses a human body but an eagle's head, brilliant red wings, and razor claws. One of Garuda's special talents is the ability to identify evil men and eat them. This means Garuda is not simply a bizarre-looking bird, but a symbol of the idea that those who commit evil acts must expect punishment.

Another Hindu figure is **Hanuman,** a giant, godlike, loyal but inquisitive monkey who tries to devour the sun but is knocked back to the earth for his greed. No one who hears about Hanuman can fail to grasp the warning about biting off more than one can chew. Hanuman's and Garuda's full stories are extremely complex, but even these brief excerpts hint at the depth and purpose built into their characters.

Indian mythology is not alone in its complexity. Greek, Roman, Chinese, Irish, Native American, and many other mythologies also run the entire gamut of human expression. Their legendary beasts, from the snake-haired lady of ancient Greece, **Medusa,** to the screaming **thunderbird** of North America, embody the most important ideas and teachings.

Not all beasts live in the musty past. Some so-called mythical creatures are still being sighted today. Modern reports of a winged humanoid dubbed **Mothman** in West Virginia and **Man Bat** in Wisconsin recall Greek creatures such as the winged **harpies**. Modern film and literature often repeat these mythical icons; the flying monkeys in the 1938 film *The Wizard of Oz* look like a cross between harpies and Hanuman the giant monkey.

The wildly popular *Harry Potter* novels by J.K. Rowling have also renewed public interest in a whole menagerie of classic, mythical beasts from three-headed dogs (**Cerberus** to the Greeks, "Fluffy" to Potter fans) to **hippogriffs** (part horse, part bird of prey). Even highly regarded cable TV networks like the *History Channel* have produced shows such as *Monsterquest*, a series that explores everything from Bigfoot to werewolves and employs scientific gadgets and methods to follow their trails.

Some mythical creatures do not look monstrous at all. A whole new generation searching for spirituality in nature has taken up the quest to discover whether "little people," or fairies, still cavort in the few undisturbed forests that remain on this planet. The Internet teems with sites devoted to fairy lore, ogres, dragons, and other creatures popularized in the 1970s by role-playing games such as *Dungeons and Dragons* and the fantasy literature explosion spearheaded by J.R.R. Tolkien's *Lord of the Rings* trilogy.

This book will trace the footsteps of all manner of legendary entities, bizarre animals and humanoids, swimming rivers after **mermaids**, and chasing giants through their mountain dens. It will peer into the past to see where some of them may have been birthed and surf contemporary media and science to compare them to modern wonders and anomalies.

Trying to sort them into some kind of order is no easy task. A **griffin**, part lion and part eagle, could fit into a chapter on animal mixtures or one concerned with strange flying things. A **centaur**, half man and half horse, might be considered a horse-beast or a human-animal hybrid. At the risk of upsetting any leftover spirits of the ancients, creatures in this book will be found in the chapter the author judges closest to their dominant trait.

Even more difficult was the task of selecting which fabulous beasts should be included. Since so much of the literature and art of the Western world is based on Greek and Roman mythology, an abundance of Greco-Roman creatures inhabit every chapter. A representative sampling from other cultures, countries, and eras rounds out each category to hint at the great variety of legends of strange creatures found worldwide.

There is also the troublesome truth that one person's myth may be another's devout belief. No disrespect is meant to anyone's religion; for the purpose of this book the term *mythical creatures* merely implies a being of legend or tradition with attributes such as giant size, impossible anatomy, or supernatural powers not found in ordinary animals or people.

A note of warning: If a few of these beasts should escape the boundaries of these pages to grab at the sun as if it were a ripened peach, or to present a face that can turn the unwary reader to stone, do not be surprised. Mythological creatures are as unpredictable as their mundane, living counterparts, and possess magical powers as well. As their histories will reveal, they have survived for eons and will probably outlive every brave reader of this book. Such is their nature and their mysterious purpose.

Mixed-Up Monsters

In a time when giant gods ruled the earth, a massive serpent named **Typhon** cast furtive glances around the world with eyes that spewed fire and decided he would be king of all. But someone else already held that title: mighty Zeus, Greek god of the sky. A battle was in the stars, and soon it was under way.

The fight was long and desperate, with many attacks and retreats on both sides. During one break in the action, Typhon mated with half-woman, half-serpent **Echidne**, and she bore him a fearfully monstrous daughter, the **Chimera** (or Chimaera). Although a thunderbolt from Zeus' arsenal finally found its mark in Typhon's scaly coils and destroyed him, Typhon had managed to father a creature as terrifying as himself.

The Chimera not only breathed fire, she could claw and bite with the head and forepaws of a lion. She inherited Typhon's lashing, dragon tail, while her midsection was like that of a goat. In fact, Chimera meant "she-goat" in ancient Greek.[1] The king of Caria captured the Chimera and kept her as a dangerous pet, but she was too powerful to contain. Unleashed, she scorched the countryside of Lycia (modern-day Turkey) with her breath and devoured all the humans she could find.

Luckily for the land's rapidly dwindling inhabitants, the hero **Bellerophon** and his flying horse, **Pegasus**, sped to the rescue and fought the grisly creature by flying above her grasp and showering her with arrows. To Bellerophon's dismay most of the arrows glanced off the Chimera's hide and only further enraged her. Bellerophon finally ran out of arrows and was left with one weapon, his giant metal spear. As he urged Pegasus to fly closer to the monster, the Chimera jumped and roared at him, searing Pegasus' hooves and feet. As the Chimera leaped her highest, Bellerophon drove the spear deep into the monster's throat. The Chimera choked and rolled, her internal fires melting the weapon until hot iron flowed into her lungs and stomach and killed her.

The Chimera was gone, but she has never been forgotten. Historians have debated the meaning and importance of the multipart creature ever since.

David Adams Leeming, a University of Connecticut scholar, believes that the killing of the she-beast by Bellerophon symbolized the Greeks' move from a goddess-worshipping society to one dominated by a male god, Zeus.[2] But the idea of the Chimera persisted beyond the culture of the early Greeks, and artists portrayed the Chimera in artworks right into Renaissance times. It graced Greek pottery as early as 650 BCE and popped up in a painting by Peter Paul Rubens in the early 1600s.

As time passed and fewer people regarded the Chimera as an actual creature, her name came to mean either a being made up of parts of different creatures or any imaginary, impossible thing—a chimera. Her patchwork pedigree was not uncommon when it came to early monster lore.

FACES OF THE SPHINX: STRANGLER AND RIDDLER

The ancient Egyptians were masters of the creature combo long before the Greeks ever put lion and goat together. Their most famous monster was probably the sphinx, which is actually a later, Greek word meaning "strangler" (in Greek mythology the sphinx strangled its victims). The sphinx is a prime and early example of a **zoomorph**, or godlike being with animal characteristics, as it possessed the head of a man and the body of a lion. Its best-known portrayal is in the giant stone monument near the pyramids of Giza known as the Great Sphinx.

Eroded by time and the elements, the Great Sphinx's true age has sparked great controversy. Its construction date has traditionally been estimated at 1400-2500 BCE. But some scholars cite geological evidence that suggest it is much older, perhaps carved as early as 10,000 BCE!

Figure 1.1 *The Sphinx and the Great Pyramid of Cheops at Giza.* (Brian Lawrence/Getty Images)

Laboratory Chimeras:
Rabbits that Glow and Pigs with Human Cells

While many cultures over the ages have believed in magically blended creatures, most modern opinion has kept the chimera securely caged in the realms of religion, myth, and fantasy. After all, it's easily observed that, with a few closely related exceptions such as the horse and donkey, animals of different species are unable to mate and produce offspring.

The new science of genetics, however, has overturned the rules of reproduction. The result is an ever-growing number of true chimeras tumbling from petri dishes in laboratories worldwide. And like many of the Greek and Egyptian gods, some are part human.

Medically speaking, a chimera combines DNA from at least two species within one body. In 1997 some media outlets mistakenly reported this had been accomplished when an ingenious University of Massachusetts medical team used cow cartilage to grow a structure shaped like a human ear on the back of a mouse. They implanted the "ear" between the mouse's skin and muscle, where it continued to grow as a graft. The result looked startling, indeed, but the process left the mouse's DNA unchanged, and thus no chimera was created.

The Chinese were the first to create human/animal chimeras, combining human cells with rabbit eggs in Shanghai in 2003. The resulting rabbit-human embryos were used to produce stem cells for medical purposes, but were not allowed to mature into full-blown "rumans" (or "habbits").[3]

Others have since attempted to make a variety of chimeras hoping to grow human organs in the new creatures, or to use them for medical research. Researchers at the Mayo Clinic in Minnesota produced pigs with human blood in 2004. In March 2007 a professor at the University of Nevada announced he had grown a human-sheep chimera that contained enough human organs inside its very sheep-like body to declare the animal 15 percent human.[4] The professor, Esmail Zanjani, had intended to grow donor-compatible organs for transplants.

Genetically engineered chimeras even rocked the world of art in 2000 when Eduardo Kac, a professor at the School of the Art Institute of Chicago, announced he had created a rabbit with jellyfish genes that gave it a green glow under ultraviolet lights. He called his project the "GFP (green fluorescent protein) Bunny" and said that two French scientists helped him with the technical end.

Art critics everywhere acclaimed the GFP Bunny; the *San Francisco Weekly* called it "both a science and art experiment."[5] But the expected exhibit of the famed rabbit, named Alba, never happened. Kac claimed that the French laboratory involved in Alba's creation, the French National Institute for Argonomic Research, refused to release the animal to him.

Genetic scientists continue to blur the borders between species; two tropical fishes, the Rosy barb and the Zebra danio, were combined into a chimera species at Ocean University of China in 2004. Some combinations have been patented even when no actual chimeras were produced.

In 2005 a New York scientist, Stuart Newman, applied for a patent on a human-ape chimera and was rejected because the creature would be "too closely related to a human to be patentable."[6] Newman was actually happy the patent was denied. His intent was to fail and set a precedent so that others would be prevented from receiving patents on living creatures.

The chimera controversy, especially when it involves human and animal genes, is likely to continue. In June 2008 a group of Catholic bishops in England and Wales told the British Parliament that human-animal chimera embryos should not be destroyed before birth but should have the right to live and be treated like other humans.[7]

Perhaps the stories of the ancient Egyptians and Greeks were prophetic in ways their creators could never have imagined.

Since this estimate predates present knowledge of the earth's earliest civilizations by several thousand years, it has been vigorously debated among scientists. Regardless, it can definitely be said that the Great Sphinx is one of man's most ancient, surviving monuments.

Scholars do agree that statues of similar human-headed creatures, such as one whose face depicts Egyptian ruler Hetepheres II, existed circa 2500 BCE, or at least 1,000 years earlier than the latest traditional construction date. Since the human faces of Egyptian sphinx sculptures often portrayed their leaders, the creature most likely symbolized the idea of a god-king.

The Egyptians had invented other types of sphinx centuries earlier. Their oldest artwork shows lions with the heads of rams and hawks, and they began depicting these monsters or "fantastic animals" on royal and ceremonial objects around 3100 BCE. One often-repeated motif was the **serpopard**, a creature with a falcon head, a snake-like neck, the body of a leopard, and wings.[8]

The Riddler

The sphinx was known in another cradle of early civilization, Sumeria, at about the same time the Egyptians began invoking its power. Rather than regarding the sphinx as a deity or god-king, the Sumerians saw the sphinx as an evil being, related to other monsters like scorpion-men or dragons.

By the time the sphinx made its way into Greek mythology, it had mutated. To the Greeks, the sphinx was a female and a trickster possessing the added advantage of wings. She guarded the city of Thebes by permitting entrance only to those who could correctly guess a riddle and promptly devoured anyone lacking the wits to do so. That included everyone but a clever man named Oedipus, who considered the question, "What speaks with one voice, walks on four feet in the morning, two feet in the afternoon and three feet in the evening?" He answered, "Man." The answer was correct because babies crawl on all fours, mature adults walk upright, and the elderly walk with a cane.

His victory so distressed the monster that she dove off the nearest cliff and perished on the rocks below.

Man-headed Manticore

Another sphinx-like creature that migrated from ancient Mesopotamia to medieval Europe was the **manticore,** first described for the Western world by Greek physician Mnemon around 400 BCE. While the manticore kept the classic sphinx's lion body with human head, it gained wings and a spiny-tipped tail that shot barbed stingers. Three rows of teeth gave it extra chewing power for crunching its victims. Its name was probably derived from an ancient Persian phrase for "man-slayer," and it was sometimes used in medieval Europe either as an allegory of the **devil** or to symbolize the prophet Jeremiah.

Figure 1.2 *The manticora, or manticore, has a lion's body, a human head, three rows of teeth, wings, and spike-tipped tail. This artist's rendition leaves the wings off the mythical beast.* (Fortean Picture Library)

Heroic Horses:
Pegasus to Unicorns

My wings are great sails, with feathers big as palm fronds, and I beat them viciously at the sky as I flee from the death of my master, Perseus. I, Pegasus, the mightiest of steeds, could not save Perseus from his half-brother, Megapenthes, and now I seek only the harshest of landscapes to mirror my grief. The rivers of Mount Helicon, home of the Muses, have all gone dry; there I shall go to mourn.

In this land I can gnash my teeth and whinny long and loud for Perseus. The grass here has dried from root to stem and the trees are bare skeletons. As I touch the scorched earth where fresh streams once poured from underground springs, I stamp my heavy hooves. As I tear at the ground, I hear the lovely nymphs, the Muses cry, too.

But no, the Muses do not cry, they laugh. Enraged, I turn to put an end to their mockery until I see that they laugh for joy. The deep prints from my hooves have brought up new springs, and the river flows again. They call this place the "Hippocrene," the Horse Spring. Even my plan for mourning has gone awry. And now I hear the voice of the goddess Athena calling me.

Although I vowed that no man should again master me, Athena has given the hero Bellerophon a golden bridle, and I cannot resist its soothing charms. I must allow Bellerophon to ride me, and together we fly to kill the monster, Chimera. Because I can soar high above the creature, Bellerophon spears it without being harmed. I feel sympathy for Chimera, since I came from such a monster myself. My mother was the snake-headed Medusa, and my father was Poseidon, god of the sea.

Now Bellerophon has spurred me to take him high into the clouds in pursuit of Mount Olympus, home of the gods. I know he is wrong to trespass there, but I am powerless to resist. I can already see the tops of the fine white towers gleaming in the light of the sun. But suddenly, a fierce pain alarms me; it is a gadfly, stinging me under my tail. The tiny devil must have been sent by Zeus, who gave it magical power to bite as no earthly insect could. I writhe and buck in torment, and as we reach the heavenly castle gate, Bellerophon tumbles from my back. He hurtles to earth, and so my second master has gone to his grave. The gate to Mount Olympus opens; Zeus bids me welcome. He sends his grooms to brush my lathered coat and tend to the gadfly wound, and tells me I belong to his own stable. I am overjoyed. I was never meant for mortal riders, and now my true master has claimed me. I, Pegasus, belong to the gods, and shall gallop the sky forever in the constellation that bears my name.

SKY STEEDS OF THE WORLD

The legend of Pegasus and other stories of Greek mythology date from at least the time of the poet Homer, who is believed to have lived around 700 BCE. Pegasus is not the only mythic horse in Greek legend; a more horrific breed of giant equines appears in the story of the **Mares of Diomedes,** who were four giant mares that belonged to the giant, Diomedes. These four massive horses were fierce eaters of human flesh and had to be tied to a bronze manger to keep them from running away and devouring the populace.

The hero Heracles (Hercules to the Romans) set out to steal the four mares as one of 12 tasks thought impossible by the gods. He accomplished the feat by killing Diomedes, and then feeding the giant's flesh to the horses to calm them. According to legend, the great

Figure 2.1 *Bellerophon rides Pegasus and slays the Chimera.* (Ivy Close Images/Landov)

warhorse of the conqueror of the Persian Empire, Alexander the Great, was descended from these mares.

Winged or giant horses often show up as companions to the gods in ancient art of Europe and the Near East.[1] A **Thracian** helmet from around 400 BCE, for instance, shows a "rider god" seated on his beautifully outfitted mount.[2] Almost as common as the winged or giant horse, and perhaps even older, is the fabled one-horned horse, or unicorn.

THE UNCANNY UNICORN

A favorite of modern fairytales and a staple of romantic fantasy, the unicorn is as familiar today as it was to people thousands of years ago. People who were children in the 1980s and early 1990s may remember Fizzy and Galaxy, unicorns in the animated series *My Pretty Pony* that was based on the best-selling Hasbro toy of the same name. Today's unicorn fans can visit a Web site called Unicorns.com[3] that offers representations of big-eyed, white unicorns in everything from jewelry to garden statues.

Proving that unicorns also trotted through human imaginations in the distant past, images of the one-horned beast have been found on hundreds of clay seals from Moenjo-Daro, a civilization that existed near present-day Pakistan around 2500 BCE. An earlier, Chaldean (Babylonian) artwork from about 3500 BCE[4] shows a unicorn fighting a lion. But depictions of ancient unicorns often looked far different than the dreamy versions favored by modern artists.

The earliest unicorns did not resemble horses but were derived from a variety of animals that included goats, oxen, gazelle, and the wild ass or onager. A Chinese version of unicorn called the **ki-lin** was described in the fourteenth century CE as an animal like a bull but with a single, curved horn. It was also sometimes believed to contain stag, horse, and deer parts, making it more chimera than unicorn. Anyone lucky enough to see a ki-lin could expect good fortune. Variations of the ki-lin exist throughout Asiatic culture.

Its appearance also signified that a great person was about to be born, and according to legend, a ki-lin showed itself to the mother of Chinese sage Confucius before his birth. It was also said to have bowed before Mongol conqueror Genghis Khan to warn him against invading India.

The Near East had its own unique unicorn, the **karkadann**. Arabian tales of the karkadann, which looked like a large type of antelope, usually revolve around hunters fighting this skilled and courageous beast. The lands inhabited by the karkadann were also home to a known antelope, the oryx. The two horns of an oryx align so perfectly when

Figure 2.2 *The ki-lin, or Chinese unicorn, has several variations in Asiatic culture. Its appearance was said to signify that a great person was going to be born.* (Nathan Godfrey)

seen from the side that many researchers believe mistaken sightings of the oryx started the karkadann lore. In the same way, the rhinoceros, the only quadruped with a naturally occurring single horn, may have sparked legends of unicorns in India.

Despite early resemblance to wild bulls and rhinos, unicorns have generally been associated with positive qualities such as good fortune, power, gentleness, and beauty. One reason for the creature's sterling reputation is that the King James Version of the Bible contains several references to unicorns. The mentions also give unicorns a permanent place in Western literature.

Biblical Unicorns

One Bible-related legend contends that the unicorn was too high-spirited to ride on Noah's ark with the other animals and that is how it became extinct. "The Unicorn," a popular 1967 song by the Irish Rovers with lyrics by Shel Silverstein, insisted the unicorns were too busy playing to make it onto the ark. Some scholars think that the word *unicorn* in verses such as Psalm 92:10: ("But my horn shalt thou exalt like the horn of the unicorn; I shall be anointed with fresh oil"), was a mistranslation. The original Hebrew word *re'em* actually meant some type of unknown animal, but was mistakenly read as "one-horned."[5]

Inspired by no fewer than seven verses about unicorns in the Old Testament, medieval Christians began to portray it in their tapestries and paintings. The unicorn came to signify Jesus Christ. Artists usually showed it as a pure white horse or goat with a long, straight spiraling horn projecting straight out from the forehead, similar to today's standard version. But there is a reason that the unicorn's horn, once always shown as thick and curved like a rhino's, became long, straight, and spiraled.

Hunting the Horn

Sometime before the end of the first millennium CE, Europeans began finding "unicorn horns" and grinding them into medicinal powder or making cups believed to neutralize poison. The horns, also known as **alicorn**, measured an average of eight feet long and were formed with a beautiful, tapering swirl. It's easy to see how people might have hoped and believed these had fallen from the noble forehead of a unicorn.

Unfortunately, they had not. In 1638 a scholar named Ole Wurm proved that the cast-off horns came from a little-known species of Arctic whale, the narwhal.[6] Still, it took at least three centuries for the knowledge of their true origin to seep into public awareness, and narwhal horns are still part of some European museum collections. Today's English coat of arms acknowledges the power of the one-horned creature with a lion and a unicorn locked in eternal combat.

It is also a testament to the power of the unicorn myth that in many places, people have attempted to create their own unicorns when none were to be found in the wild. As far back as the middle of the first century CE, a Roman scholar named Pliny the Elder described a method of twisting the two horns of an ox together by using boiling wax to make them pliable.

Do-it-Yourself Unicorns

Kaffir tribesmen in Africa also created faux-cattle unicorns in the late 1700s, if reports by a French traveler named LeVaillant are to be believed.[7] The major breakthrough came in 1933 when Dr. W. Franklin Dove carried out an experiment on a calf at the University of Maine. He was able to transplant the calf's small buds of tissue that would later mature into horns so that they were side by side in the middle of its forehead. By the age of two and a half, the calf had a large, formidable single horn that seemed to give it an advantage over other young bulls. Dr. Dove published an article on his work in 1936, and the modern world beheld a photo of a **bovine** unicorn.

Dr. Dove was not the last person to create his own unicorn. His one-horned calf did not in the least resemble the lovely white creatures of medieval artwork, so a married couple named Diane "Morning Glory" and Timothy "Otter" (now Oberon) Zell undertook their own project using an Angora goat.

In 1980 the Zells (also known then as the G'Zells and now as the Ravenheart-Zells) released photos of a stunning white goat named Lancelot who sported a 10-inch-long single horn. With feathery, fringed fur, beard, flowing tail, and cloven hooves, Lancelot bore a close resemblance to the medieval ideal, which was sometimes portrayed as a goat. Lancelot eventually wound up as an exhibit in the Ringling Brothers and Barnum and Bailey Circus. Although the Zells refused to tell exactly how his horn was created, later medical tests showed it was the result of a simple grafting technique similar to Dove's. It may be the closest thing to a living unicorn the modern world will ever see.

HORSES OF DIFFERENT COLORS: OTHER EQUINE MONSTERS

Although winged horses and unicorns are the most prominent mythical creatures associated with horses, lesser-known equine monsters abound. Besides Pegasus, the Greeks also had their **hippocamp**, or "waterhorse." This hybrid's front end looked like a horse, but its rear was like a sea serpent's tail. It competed for sea dominance with the **hydrippus**, a horse/fish combo.

In China the **oni** is a demon with horns and either the head of a horse or an ox. These creatures are three-eyed, multicolored, leave three-toed

The Human Unicorn

Stashed among jars of pickled tumors and cases filled with deformed skeletons at the strange Mütter Museum in Philadelphia, Pennsylvania, is a wax model of the head of a French woman, Madame DiManche. The woman, who made her living in the early nineteenth century as a laundress, was included in the collection of physical oddities because from her forehead grew a thick, 10-inch horn! She was known around Paris as Mére la Corne, or "Mother Horn."

The horn was so heavy that it had to be supported by a sling attached to her nightcap. It was not a classic, graceful unicorn horn, either; it curved downward over her face. She lived with the startling nuisance for about six years, then finally allowed surgeons to cut it off when she was almost 80. Madame DiManche explained that she thought the horn looked like a mark of the devil and didn't want to appear at the heavenly gates looking as if she belonged somewhere else.[8]

The woman lived at least four more years, horn free. Several wax and plaster models had been made of her face and appendage before footprints, and are associated with illness, death, and disease. One of their tasks is to ferry people to the underworld in fiery chariots.

Scotland's mythic equine is called the **waterhorse**, with several varieties to watch out for. Most famous was the kelpie, a shape-shifter that most often appeared near rivers or lakes in the form of a beautiful horse. It was said no traveler could resist the urge to mount the graceful beast but would soon find himself carried into deep water and, usually, drowned. A more vicious form of kelpie, the **ech-ushkya**, resembled ponies but devoured their victims after drowning them.[11] The Irish version is known as a **pooka (phouka)**, and its appearance is always a bad omen.

---

the horn was removed, and one ended up in the Mütter Museum. The museum's collection also boasts a similar, 12-inch horn taken from a 70-year-old woman.

Dermatologists call these weird facial features **cutaneous horns**, meaning that they grew from skin cells run amok. Cutaneous horns are very rare in humans, but proof of their existence has also popped up in places like the Museum of Edinburgh University. Its collection includes a horn a few inches long cut in 1671 from a 50-year-old woman named Elizabeth Love.[9] Also, a London newspaper of the 1700s described how a London surgeon removed a three-inch growth resembling a ram's horn from a woman's forehead. According to C.J.S. Thompson's *The Mystery and Lore of Monsters*, the horn was presumed by the reporter to be a "supernatural production."[10]

Small cutaneous horns, usually no more than half an inch long, are sometimes discovered growing out of people's hands and feet, and occasionally from a nostril. They occur in both men and women. Some are cancerous but most are not. The peak age for cutaneous horns is between 60 and 70.

Odin, king of Germanic deities, rode an eight-legged horse named **Sleipnir.**[12] Not limited to hoofing it on land, Sleipnir's octopedic gallop carried him over water or through the air with equal ease. Like most mythic creatures he was of very mixed parentage; his mother was a shape-shifter named Loki (masquerading as a mare) and his father was a magically strong stallion, Svadilfari.

Probably one of the most fantastic examples of mythic horse creatures was the **centicore,** or **yale**, a spotted horse-like animal with a goat head and elephant tail. Although first described by Pliny the Elder, the lore of the yale survived into medieval and later times. Its strangest attribute was its ability to rotate its two horns strategically for battle. British writer Sir Arthur Shipley believed the concept of this creature originated in ancient Egypt, with its name derived from the Hebrew word for mountain goat, *ya' el.*[13] Wherever it came from, the yale has been immortalized in carvings on several college campus buildings in Cambridge, England.

Fabled Flyers

The autumn air on the night of September 26, 2006, was chill. At about 9 p.m., darkness cloaked the country lane called Briggs Road just outside of LaCrosse, Wisconsin, a town known for its choice location on the Mississippi River. A 55-year-old man and his 25-year-old son kept a close eye on the road ahead of them as they crested a hill and approached a private shooting range on the right side of Briggs Road. Suddenly, something huge flew straight at the windshield of their pickup truck. Both men were sure it was going to hit them. But just before impact, it sailed straight up and off into the night. Father and son both had a very good look at the creature at close range, and what they saw astonished them.

It was some sort of flying beast, with bat-like wings that spanned about 10 feet. At the center of the wings hung a human-sized, six-to seven-foot tall, furred creature with an almost canine head, sharp fangs, and a long tail. Its arms and legs ended in claws, and as it sailed away, it uttered a long, piercing shriek that shook the men to their core. They both became sick almost immediately, and the son had to pull the car over to retch. The father, who preferred to release only his Cherokee name of *Wohali* to the public, was ill for the entire week following the incident. The men told their story to a relative who contacted this author.[1]

Wohali drew a sketch of his impression of the creature, adding notes that included these remarks: "It seemed really angry, like we surprised it . . . I remember the teeth and the scream we heard was terrifying. It looked hungry."

FEATHER-PHOBIA

Wohali and his son are not the first humans to have been terrorized by a flying menace. Men have gazed at the sky with fearful trepidation for eons. The ancient Assyrians believed in an evil demigod named **Pazuzu,** who bears some resemblance to the LaCrosse Man Bat.

Author D.J. Conway describes Pazuzu as a "winged demon genie of the first millennium BCE" in his book, *Magical Mystical Creatures.*[2] Like the Man Bat, Pazuzu possessed a canine-like face. Conway notes that in one depiction dating from about 1000-800 BCE, Pazuzu is shown with four wings and bird-like feet.[3] He also appears with clawed, lion paws and is the representative of storms and disease. The latter is an interesting detail, considering that the two men who observed the La-Crosse Man Bat instantly became ill.

FLYING GOBLINS OF GREECE

The Greeks also had dire reason to keep looking up. Harpies, or "Snatchers" (from the Greek *harpazein*, "to snatch"), were woman-birds associated, like Pazuzu, with storms. It was their job to snatch away those who made the gods angry, and they usually worked in squadrons of three. Although from the torso up they looked like young women, their fingers ended in great claws and their bodies were like giant vultures. When bored or hungry, they would swoop down to steal food from unwary picnickers and then stuff themselves. This was always followed by a foul vomiting session, directed at those whose feast they had stolen.

Greeks also had to watch out for **sirens**, another type of malevolent, bird-bodied woman that were originally depicted with beards.[4] Like birds, they sang beautifully and were known to lure men to death with their alluring melodies. They could be defeated by plucking their

Figure 3.1   *The ancient Assyrian demon Pazuzu was associated with storms and disease. Pazuzu had a dog-like face, four wings, and bird-like claws.* (Gianni DagliOrti/Corbis)

feathers or avoided by plugging one's ears. The poet Homer wrote in *The Odyssey*, ". . . he's enchanted by the clear, sweet songs of the Sirens, who sit in a meadow, surrounded by a great heap of rotting men . . ."[5]

Another menace of Grecian skies was the **Stymphalian bird,** named for its habitat around the city of Stymphalus. These creatures were dangerous, even from afar, since they could shoot individual feathers as if they were arrows. Their beaks and talons were made of bronze, and they loved to dine on human flesh. The Greek hero Heracles (Hercules) defeated the Stymphalian birds after he discovered they could be frightened by the sound of a metal rattle and that they became vulnerable to man-made arrows as they fled.

NORTH AMERICAN AND AFRICAN SKY SCREECHERS

Another ancient storm-bringer was the Native American thunderbird, known to many tribes across North America. Giant spirit birds whose wings make thunder and whose eyes flash lightning, they have the power to whip up great storms. Their natural enemy is the horned water serpent, and among some Alaskan tribes the thunderbird may also snatch away people and animals.[6]

Another giant bird-creature of indigenous Americans is the **piasa**. A restored rock painting on a cliff outside of Alton, Illinois, shows it as a winged, claw-footed monster with antlers, huge fangs, and a long, skinny tail. The Illiniwek people who created the artwork said that it preferred human flesh as food, and in 1836 an explorer named John Russell discovered a cave full of human bones in the same area as the painting. Russell concluded from this that the man-eating bird really existed,[7] but others have pointed out there is no evidence connecting the bones to the piasa.

Flying monsters are not limited to the indigenous people of the western world. East Africans have long kept careful watch for the **chemosit,** half bird and half man, and also fond of human flesh. What makes the chemosit truly unusual in the big bird pantheon is that it has no fewer than nine sets of buttocks.

THE PHOENIX AND FRIENDS

J.K. Rowlings' fictional *Harry Potter* series brought many ancient, mythical creatures to public attention, and one of them was Professor Dumbledore's pet **phoenix**, a bird that would burst into flame and then rise again from its own ashes. Physically similar to a heron but with red and gold feathers, it can be traced back to ancient Egypt, and various legends place its lifespan between 500 and 1,000 years.

Greek writers adopted the fabulous bird enthusiastically as early as 800 BCE, and similar birds appear in other cultures, often connected with the sun. The Chinese believed a fiery-hued creature called the *feng-huang* came to them from the sun. And one of the most famous versions comes from Russia in the popular ballet, *The Firebird*, by Igor Stravinsky.[8]

The white-feathered **roc** of Arabia is quite different than the phoenix. It is big enough to hoist an elephant and lays eggs like massive boulders. The roc first appears in tales of both ancient China and Arabia, described as being built like a huge eagle. The earliest story of a roc-like bird enters literary history in the fourth century BCE in ancient tales of India. It was usually seen as helpful and benevolent to humans. As late as the early 1300s, explorer Marco Polo described the roc as part of the **fauna** of Madagascar.

AIRBORNE ANIMALS

Not all legendary flyers are bird or bat. One of the most ancient, the griffin or gryphon, consists of a lion's body with wings and eagle's beak added. Derived from ancient chimeras such as the Egyptian sphinx, images of griffin-like animals predate written language in many cultures and date back at least 5,000 years.[9]

The griffin is most often described as noble but ferocious, and its name was probably taken from the Latin *gryphus*, which means "to

Figure 3.2 *The phoenix rises from the flames.* (Caren Loebel-Fried/Getty Images)

seize." Although it kept its basic lion/eagle makeup wherever it was found, each culture gave the creature its own style of head ornament. A survey of griffins in art through the ages reveals griffins topped with knobs, crests, wavy manes, or crowns, depending on their country of origin.

A Greek writer named Aristeas, from about 800 BCE, made the first known written reference to griffins when he told of a one-eyed tribe of men in Central Asia. The tribe's chief aim was to steal gold guarded by monsters that sounded so much like the griffins Aristeas knew from Greek tradition that he bestowed the name upon them in a poem.[10] From then on, griffins were often regarded as guardians of treasure. Later legends even insisted that griffin nests were woven from gold.

Like the unicorn, griffins were sometimes used as a symbol of Christ (the poet Dante was best known for this) and became one of the most popular figures used on medieval coats-of-arms.

One scholar, Horace Wilson, has suggested the griffin's closest cousins may be two giant birds of India, either the sacred bird-deity Garuda or the giant called **Gold-Maker,** which could create gold by mixing its own droppings with sand.[11]

Another relative of the griffin is the hippogriff, a creature with the rear quarters of a horse added to the lion and eagle mix. An inhabitant of remote mountain regions, the hippogriff was a popular entry in **bestiaries** of medieval Europe, and it became well known after playing a big role in the adventure poem, *Orlando Furioso*, by Italian writer Ludvico Ariosto around 1500 CE.

BASILISK BASICS

Sorting out the various monster blends that have occurred over time can be confusing, and one of the most puzzling creatures is the **basilisk**, part serpent and part rooster, which gained a rooster's head and a new name, the **cockatrice,** in medieval times.

To the ancient Egyptians, the basilisk was actually a type of cobra able to kill any type of plant, landscape, or creature with its breath. Associated with royalty because of its upright posture and a white, crown-like marking on its head, the kingly snake evolved into a winged monster by the Middle Ages, roughly the fifth to fifteenth centuries CE.

The serpent-lizard had merged with the rooster at least by 1218 CE, however, when a popular bestiary described a type of animal that grew from an egg formed in the body of a rooster and hatched by a toad, so that it retained parts of each. This bestiary also mentioned that a mirror could be used as a protective shield while hunting the creature, as any fan of the Harry Potter series will remember reading in *Harry Potter and the Chamber of Secrets*. However, according to medieval legend, another good protection against

New Jersey's Flying Devil

Of all the mythical winged monsters in history, only one is described as a kangaroo with wings. Although a flying kangaroo sounds more comical than humorous, the **Jersey Devil** has terrorized a large swath of two states for centuries.

In 1909 people in at least 30 different towns in Pennsylvania and New Jersey reported seeing a large, bat-winged creature with a head like a ram and a penetrating scream. Its footprints appeared to be made by hooves rather than talons. Some likened it to the medieval **gargoyle**, a flying monster often depicted on waterspouts or perched as a guardian sculpture on cathedrals or other large buildings.

As sightings intensified during the week of January 16-23, 1909, a whole trolley load of people saw the thing in Haddon Heights, New Jersey, and agreed it resembled a winged kangaroo.[12] Search teams went out with bloodhounds, schools were closed, and people in the New Jersey area called the Pine Barrens were afraid to travel. People reported pets killed and livestock missing.

Well into the twenty-first century, people still claimed to encounter the creature in the Pine Barrens. In the spring of 2007, a pair of campers in Sussex County reported they were followed by a tall, black figure whose basilisks was to carry a weasel, the only animal immune to the basilisk's deadly powers.

Today, the creature's name has reverted to reptile status. The basilisk of the natural world is a mild-mannered South American lizard, no more than two and one-half feet long. Far from the devilish reputation of its mythical counterpart, it is nicknamed the "Jesus Christ" lizard for its ability to walk on water using long, paddle-like scales on the outsides of its toes.

---

footsteps sounded like the hooves of an ox, according to a Web site devoted to the Jersey flyer, LandoftheDevil.com.[13] But it is understandable that the monster has become so entrenched in local lore, considering that its history dates back to the area's earliest settlers.

The legend actually began in 1735, when Deborah Leeds of Atlantic County, New Jersey, became pregnant with her 13th child. Because the family lived in extreme poverty, the woman was said to have cursed the babe in her womb, asking God to make it a devil. The baby turned into a hideous demon as soon as it was born, killing the mother, midwives, and other family members before making its escape into the Pine Barrens, where it lurked until something stirred it into its rampage in 1909.

Area historians think the story may have a more logical origin and that perhaps Mrs. Leeds gave birth to a physically deformed child. As it grew and was glimpsed by neighbors, they eventually exaggerated its appearance into that of a monster. The creature is still known as the Leeds Devil to inhabitants of the Pine Barrens.[14]

The Jersey Devil will not soon be forgotten, whether it continues to make public appearances or stays put in its woodland home. It has played lead character in a number of books and movies, the state's NHL hockey team is named after it, as is a Playstation video game, and the creature is now a very popular entity on Internet monster sites.

MOTHMAN, WEST VIRGINIA'S HARBINGER OF DESTRUCTION

Although most people would probably prefer to leave giant monster-birds safely in the past, new versions of mythic winged things, such as the LaCrosse Man Bat, keep cropping up. Before the Man Bat, there was Mothman, a large, winged figure that haunted West Virginia's Ohio Valley area in 1966 and 1967.

The epicenter of the sightings occurred in a small town called Mount Pleasant. The phenomenon's chief investigator, John Keel, said that he interviewed hundreds of witnesses during those years.[15] Witness accounts varied slightly, but the most usual description was a grayish, humanoid creature with 10-foot, bat-like wings, a head that blended straight into the body, and large, red eyes.

Since several sightings were recorded in the days immediately before December 15, 1967, when the bridge over the Ohio River at Point Pleasant collapsed and killed 46 people, some think Mothman may have appeared as a foreteller of doom. Whatever it was, Mothman has been the subject of several books, documentaries, and a 2002 feature film, *The Mothman Prophecies*, starring Richard Gere.

AIRBORNE FROM OTHER ERAS

As outlandish as the idea of giant, weird birds may seem, there are a few known creatures that may have sparked sightings from ancient times to present. One of the most impressive is the now-extinct **Washington eagle**, a russet-brown sea eagle with a 10-foot wingspan sighted by a number of early American naturalists.

Its most famous witness was John James Audubon, still known today for his accurate and artistic paintings of birds and other wildlife. He sighted Washington eagles at least five times, starting in 1814, and shot one in Kentucky that he was able to measure and describe in detail. Washington eagles were seen by other observers around the United States in the first half of the nineteenth century.[16]

These huge birds of prey have been presumed extinct for at least 150 years, but a few relict survivors could explain many baffling modern sightings. One witness claimed that he and his wife sighted one on the Mississippi River, near Stillwater, Minnesota, in 2004.[17] (This was within easy flying range of the LaCrosse Man Bat sighting.) Could Washington eagles also account for Native American Thunderbirds?

Another airborne creature from a far more distant past is often cited as a possible culprit to explain giant bird appearances. The **pteranodon**, a flying reptile of the late Cretaceous period (90-65 million years ago), is one of a larger group of extinct creatures known as **pterosaurs.** With wingspans ranging from 20-30 feet and heads accented by pointed, bony crests, even a single pteranodon would present an awesome spectacle. Hopeful believers may wonder whether a few may have survived in some remote location, or perhaps found a time/space portal that allows them to visit us on occasion.

In 1976 a human-sized, leathery-winged creature swooped down on a Texas man, Armando Grimaldo, and attempted to carry him off. Authors Janet and Colin Bord include this story in a chapter of *Creatures from Elsewhere* titled "Flight Across Time?" with a subtitle, "Terrified witnesses have told of winged creatures that strikingly resembled pterodactyls . . ."[18]

In another instance, Dr. Bernard Heuvelmans, a French/Belgian scientist known as the "Father of Cryptozoology" (the science of hidden animals), described a large, featherless flying creature known as a **kongamato**. This was no monster from the ancient past; it had been sighted in Zambia and Rhodesia as late as the 1920s. The animal, whose name meant "boat-breaker," was known for attacking people trying to cross rivers in its territory. An explorer named Frank Melland, said Heuvelmans in *Strange Magazine*, showed Rhodesian eyewitnesses' drawings of prehistoric creatures, and they unerringly chose pteranodon-like pterodactyls as dead-on likenesses of the leathery kongamato.[19]

A legend of a pterodactyl-like thunderbird photo has circulated among cryptozoology buffs for many years. It was supposed to have been published in the *Tombstone Epitaph* in 1886, but no such picture can be found in newspaper records.[20] The paper did publish a story about a 92-foot winged creature killed by two ranchers about that same time, but newspaper articles about monsters from that era are notoriously unreliable, and were often invented to sell more papers.

Many Canadian television viewers have insisted that researcher Ivan Sanderson showed the photo on a 1970s talk show, but author Dr. Karl Shuker believes the viewers may simply remember their own visualization of Sanderson's *description* of such a picture.[21] Human memory, it seems, can be both inventive and resourceful.

Half and Half: Beast-People

Half man and half goat, the creature known as the **goatman** is as much a part of Prince George's County, Maryland, as the woods and fields in which it is said to cavort.

Its story began in the late 1700s when wealthy Marylander Thomas Snowden bought 9,000 acres northeast of Washington, D.C., and with the help of a large staff of slaves made it a prosperous tobacco plantation. When Snowden's daughter, Mary, wed, he gave her 475 acres as a wedding present. It was this little corner of Snowden's plantation that the U.S. government purchased in 1910 as the start of its main farm and agricultural research center, which now covers 6,700 acres.

The Henry A. Wallace Beltsville Agricultural Research Center (BARC) became known for its pioneering research in genetics. Its Web site says that it has received awards for its discoveries of new forms of life.[1] But did one unlucky government scientist at BARC accidentally discover the secret to becoming a goatman?

Many area residents tell the story of a BARC scientist who was said to be working on a genetic experiment on a herd of goats in the 1970s. One of the genetically altered goats bit the scientist, and its mutated saliva worked a sudden transformation upon the man. As he watched the lower half of his body change into that of a goat and felt horns curl over his forehead, brown fur sprouted on his chest and arms. He leaped in panic from the goat pen into the surrounding fields and made his way to the woods. Ever since, he has wreaked havoc on local people, pets, and livestock, often venting his madness by tearing animals' heads from their bodies.

The goatman is especially fond of searching lonely roads for parked cars occupied by teenage lovers. In one oft-repeated tale a young teen was busy fending off her love-struck prom date when they heard curious noises coming from under the car. The young man climbed out to investigate. As the girl looked out the window, she saw a six-foot-tall creature, part man and part goat, with glowing green eyes. Her date was later found torn limb from limb.

One area writer, Mark Opsasnick, investigated the goatman and included what he found in a book titled *Horror on Fletchertown Road: the Goatman of Prince George's County, Maryland.* Opsasnick interviewed farm families around the town of Bowie, which lies a few miles east of Beltsville. He discovered that some of them had used the story of the goatman as a "bogeyman" tale to keep youngsters in line for many decades. Opsasnick deduced that the story spread into area schools from the offspring of these farmers,[2] and speedily mutated into an urban legend. However, unexplained, hairy creatures on two feet are still occasionally sighted in the area to this day, according to the book, *Weird Maryland.*[3]

HEINOUS HYBRIDS

The mythic image of the goatman has butted heads with reality since the ancient Greeks told of horned, goat-legged **satyrs** that terrorized their forests. Satyrs were known as enthusiastic party animals that loved to carouse until dawn.

The son of the Greek god Hermes, **Pan**, looked much like the satyrs and although famous for playing beautiful music on his reed pipes, could pitch a frightening fit when angered. The Roman god of rural land, **Faunus**, was a sort of a cousin to Pan. His goatman offspring, the **fauns** or **fauni**, also resembled satyrs but enjoyed a more

Figure 4.1 *Legends of goatmen have circulated since the time of the ancient Greeks, who told of goat-legged satyrs lurking in their wooded areas.* (Troy Therrien)

wholesome reputation. Their one negative trait was the ability to trigger nightmares by sneaking into a human's bedroom.

The idea of combining man and beast into a single being does not stop with goats. Ancient legends overflow with a bizarre zoo of **manimals**, or half-and-half creatures.

One of the oldest ideas is that of the dog-headed man, or **cynocephali**. Dating this strain of hybrids back to the jackal-headed death god of the Egyptians, **Anubis**, author Patricia Dale-Green refers to the culture of humanized canines as "dogmanity."[4]

As early as the fifth century BCE, the Greek doctor Ctésias wrote a book about India in which he described a race of dog-headed people that cooked their prey by sun-baking it. Explorer Marco Polo also claimed around 1300 CE that a region near India's Bay of Bengal was home to a nation of cynocephali that worshipped oxen.

Old Irish legends include a tribe of dog-headed Celts called the **Concheannaich**, and as late as the Middle Ages, Greek Orthodox churches portrayed the martyr **St. Christopher** (circa 300 CE) as a dog-headed man. According to legend, the saint had prayed that God would make him ugly to keep himself from the sin of vanity. Christopher received his wish in the form of a hound's head. Although he was considered the patron saint of travelers for many years, in 1969 the Roman Catholic Church removed Christopher's feast day from its calendar due to lack of historical evidence of his existence.

Bullish Beastmen

The professional basketball team known as the Chicago Bulls may lack horns and hooves, but ancient bull-men once pawed and stamped on earth, according to various legends. The bull was one of the earliest animals depicted in human art; it is found in clay statues and wall murals of the city of Catal Hüyük, a city that flourished in what is now present-day southern Turkey around 6000 BCE.[5] Cattle were important as a food source and draft animal, and the strength and ferocity of the bull made it a natural selection for worship and ritual.

The earliest known mythic adventure poem, *The Epic of **Gilgamesh***, includes a character named **Enkidu** who was half man, half bull.[6] The story, which came from Mesopotamia around 2000 BCE, tells how the gods sent a wild, man-beast to help subdue the tyrant-king, Gilgamesh. Eventually the two became friends and battle comrades until Enkidu was killed, perhaps symbolizing man's taming of the beast within.

The most famous bull-man was probably the **Minotaur**, another product of the unusual pairings of the Greek gods. His mother was a queen of the island of Crete, and she conceived the Minotaur with a white bull sent by Poseidon from the sea. The bull-man lived in a cave surrounded by a maze called the Labyrinth, and its diet required the sacrifice of 14 girls and boys per year. Theseus was the hero finally able to end the annual teen feast. Theseus accomplished his mission by unraveling a ball of yarn to mark his trail through the maze as he tracked the Minotaur and then slew it with a sword.

One lesser-known bull-man was the **bucentaur** of Greek mythology, with the head, arms, and torso of a man growing from the four-legged body of a bull.[7]

Horsing Around

The satyrs mentioned earlier were not the only Greek beast-men to party hearty; the half-man, half-horse centaurs were also famous for nightlong revelries, usually in the region of Thessaly. Like bucentaurs, their upper parts were human but they ran on four hooved feet. The centaurs were known for downing huge quantities of wine and fresh meat.

One Greek centaur, **Chiron**, stood head and withers above the rest. Chiron's parents were both of human shape, but his father, Cronos, sired him while in the form of a horse. This unusual origin gave Chiron the body of a centaur (although sometimes he is shown in Greek artworks with human legs) but a much wiser, gentler personality than centaurs were said to possess. Shunning the wild forest life of other centaurs, Chiron made his home in a cave where he shared his vast knowledge with Greek heroes who sought his wisdom.

Scholars believe the first centaurs date back to artwork created around 1750 BCE by an ancient people, the Kassites, who were originally from the area now known as Iran.[8] The Kassites carved images of centaurs on boundary marker stones, which implies that they regarded centaurs as guardians. And two centaurs still guard the boundaries of our night sky in the constellations Centaurus and Sagittarius.

Fishy Folk

Another universal and ancient pairing of man and beast is the familiar form of mermaids and mermen (*mer* means "sea"). The first known half-human, half-fish is **Oannes**, the Babylonian sea-god who gave humankind agriculture and other arts of civilization. The ancient Syrians and Philistines worshipped a mermaid goddess named **Atargatis**[9] without whose permission fishermen could not ply their trade, but the Romans destroyed her Syrian temple in 55 BCE.[10]

The Greeks also had a race of merpeople, the **Tritons**, who were named after a son of Poseidon. Later their woman-headed birds called sirens evolved into mermaids, as explained in Chapter 3. But the Roman writer Pliny the Elder, 23-79 CE, wrote convincingly of mermaids as if they were real, saying, ". . . it is no fabulous tale that goeth of

The Devil: Myth or Monster?

One of the most familiar humanoid creatures in literature and lore is the devil, or Satan. He is usually depicted as a goatman with horns and a human form, but prancing on goat-like legs with hooves. Sometimes a barbed tail completes the picture, with red skin to represent the eternal fires of his underworld abode. He has many other names from the Bible and other literature: The Adversary, Beelzebub, Old Nick, Lucifer, and Mephistopheles are just a few.

Satan is also one of the most controversial figures in religion and philosophy. Many religious traditions regard him as an actual, living entity. Others say that he is real but only as a spirit. Some think he is merely a legendary symbol of man's lower nature.

Jewish, Islamic, and Christian traditions often describe the devil as an angel that fell from his position in Heaven after he rebelled against God. He has functioned ever since as the originator of evil, the enemy of God, and the source of man's temptation to sin. The biblical New Testament idea of a hierarchy of demons and other evil spirits under Satan's them; . . . only their bodie is rough and scaled all over, even in those parts wherein they resemble women . . ."[11]

About 600 years after Pliny's time, an Irish document claimed that in 558 CE, a fisherman caught a mermaid named Liban in his net in Lough Neagh in Ulster. Other Irish reports claim mermaids were also discovered in 887 and 1118.[12] Occasional, unverifiable accounts of mermaids have surfaced throughout Europe into modern times, with sightings in the Irish Sea's Isle of Man in 1961 and from British Columbia and South Borneo in 1967. A somewhat troubling incident occurred in 1988, when a scuba diver named Robert Foster reported that

command is similar to that found in ancient Persia's religion, Zoroastrianism, which also stated the devil had been around from the start of creation but would someday lose his position of power.[13]

Through the ages, Satan has been blamed for just about every woe to befall man. A list described by a *Funk & Wagnall's* article on the devil includes: "crop failure, sterility, pestilence, heresies, individual vices, and the whole body of heathenism with its mythology and religious worship."[14]

As busy as that may keep him, the devil does not always appear as a goatman. According to the Bible, he also "masquerades as an angel of light." According to a folk legend still circulating in rural areas of the United States, he also sometimes appears as a handsome, well-dressed stranger at barn dances.

As the American legend goes, he quickly chooses a pretty girl to whisk around the floor and proceeds to wow the crowd with his light step and quick footwork. At the end of the dance he disappears into the night. When his chosen partner goes looking for him, all she finds in the sawdust on the floor or the mud outside the barn are the prints of goat hooves. Then, to her great dismay, she realizes that she has danced with the devil.

a mermaid menaced him with "evil eyes" in Florida's coastal waters. He was able to swim away before she could do him any damage.[15]

In these instances, witnesses saw the mermaids as living beings unknown to science rather than mythical creatures. Yet, most people believe that merbeings belong firmly in the category of ancient legend. Either way, finned beauties remain popular subjects of film and fairytale. As of this writing, the Disney Corporation continues to profit from its animated film versions of Hans Christian Andersen's *The Little Mermaid*, and Denmark's Tourist Board claims Copenhagen's mermaid sculpture is the world's most-photographed statue.[16]

Elephant Man and Stomach Faces

In India, many sacred characters combine human and animal features. Hindu god **Ganesha** is portrayed in Indian art as a potbellied man with an elephant head. Ganesha combines both good and negative qualities. He is the patron of literature, having torn off one of his tusks in order to quickly pen the first copy of the epic Hindu story, *The Mahabarata*. His potbelly symbolizes a negative aspect: greed. Still, he is considered a lucky emblem for businesses, with the ability to help new ventures succeed.

Unlike most Greek manimals, he came by his elephant head not through monstrous mating, but because as a child his head was accidentally torn from his shoulders by the god Shiva. His mother, Parvati, insisted Shiva make up for the terrible deed, so Shiva replaced Ganesha's head with that of an elephant.

One of the most unusual human-animal combinations, though, is the Greek-Roman monster called the **gryllus**. Pig-men who combined the head of a porker with a second face—a human one—peering out from their stomachs, the grylli were mentioned by the Greek writer Plutarch around 100 BCE. In Plutarch's tale, the sorceress, Circe, created the creatures when she punished a group of men by making them swine-like. Their name came from the Greek verb *gryl*, meaning "to grunt."

Figure 4.2 *The round-bellied Hindu god Ganesha has the body of a man and the head of an elephant.* (Anthony Tahlier/Getty Images)

Flying Flame Shooters: Dragons of the World

The city of Silene loomed high over the desert, its thick, mud walls standing in square contrast to the curving palm trees in the surrounding oasis. One day, sometime around 300 CE, guards within the small Libyan fortress town watched suspiciously as a young man on an impressively armored mount approached.

The lone rider, George, had traveled a long way from his home in Cappadocia in present-day Turkey. As his horse picked its way along the shore of a great pond that lay below the city, George heard a pitiful wailing. He followed the sound to discover a beautiful young woman seated on a rock near the water's edge. Her richly dyed and embroidered robes implied that this was her wedding day. Puzzled, George looked about him for the groom, but saw no one.

Between sobs the woman explained her predicament. In the pond lived a giant dragon, she said, whose poison breath killed anyone it touched. The town had struck a deal with the beast to offer a sheep every week if he would leave them alone. It wasn't long before all the sheep were gone and then the rest of the livestock. Reluctantly, the townspeople began to draw lots to sacrifice their sons and daughters. The king's family was not excluded, and this week had been the unlucky "winners." The princess Cleolinda now waited for her unthinkable fate: to disappear down the monster's gullet.

Suddenly, a great splash startled the pair as the beast rose out of the lake on leathery wings. Its red eyes glittered as it waggled its long, clicking talons toward the shrieking Cleolinda. George whirled on his mount and charged the dragon. Taking deadly aim, he managed to pierce its soft belly with his lance. The creature staggered under the blow. George quickly asked Cleolinda to toss to him the fabric belt she wore around her garments.

George threw the embroidered girdle over the creature's neck, and when it touched the dragon, the beast became weaker still. George led it to the city and returned Cleolinda to her father. He then beheaded the dragon with his sword, Askalon, and the entire city converted to his faith in their gratitude.

DRAGONS OF ANTIQUITY

The story of St. George and the dragon, even though it was added to the biography of the Christian martyr hundreds of years after his death, helped to make the dragon one of the most familiar fabulous beasts of the Middle Ages and the Renaissance. George became the patron saint of England. In fact, British folklore went so far as to move the site of the slaying from Libya to England, at **Dragon Hill** near Uffington where legend says the dragon is buried.[1] Next to Dragon Hill is another hillside bearing a stylized horse or dragon from about 1000 BCE cut into the chalky bedrock. Huge, reptilian monsters have been key players in legends since the time of our most ancient civilizations.

Tiamat, a female dragon whose body began as seawater, represented power on a cosmic scale in the creation myths of the Sumerian and Babylonian people. According to the ancient document the *Enuma elish*, her body was as vast as the ocean, her skin so thick no sword could penetrate it. Formidable horns crowned her head, and she used her tail to fight enemies and whip up towering waves.

Figure 5.1   *An artist's rendering of a fire-breathing dragon.*   (Linda S. Godfrey)

Tiamat's husband, Apsu, was her freshwater counterpart, and the two of them spawned not only the sky and the earth, but countless and varied monsters. Tiamat was eventually killed by a clever offspring who rained arrows into her open mouth. Her blood flowed so furiously that it became all the rivers of the earth.[2]

Ancients of Asia

Very similar to Tiamat is the Chinese **Ti Lung**, who oversees rain and flowing waters of the world. **Lung** actually refers to a class of dragons, each with its own appearance and traits. The lung's scales, long neck, and clawed forearms are lizard-like, but its bearded head is more like that of a camel, with prominent and sometimes floppy ears. The lung prance in a rainbow of colors and may or may not fly.

The dragon is usually a symbol of happiness and good fortune in Oriental cultures. At least two ancient Chinese emperors (Hwang Ti, 2697 BCE, and Shun, 2255 BCE) were described as having faces that resembled those of dragons.[3] This was considered an admirable trait. But dragons could be changeable in appearance and playfully elusive.

An ancient Chinese document called the *Twan-ting-t'u*, quoted in Charles Gould's *Mythical Monsters*, says of the yellow dragon: ". . . He can be large or small, obscure or manifest, short or long, alive or dead; the king cannot drain the pool and catch him. His intelligence and virtue are unfathomable; moreover he assures the peaceful air, and sports in the pools."[4]

A ritual dragon dance performed with large, cloth puppets persists in modern celebrations such as weddings and the Chinese New Year festival. Along with the ki-lin (Chinese unicorn), the phoenix, and the tortoise, the dragon is still regarded as one of four sacred animals in Chinese culture. Ground-up dragon bones, usually obtained from dinosaur fossils, are sold in China as medicine.

THE CLASSICAL DRAGON

The Greek word for pythons, the largest of the serpents, was *draconta*. The Romans shortened the word to *draco*, which became the source of the English word dragon. The giant python that guarded sacred springs and hoards of gold in Greek mythology was named **Drakon**. The hero Cadmus killed Drakon by pounding his head with a rock

Figure 5.2   *A Chinese dragon floats at sea. In Chinese culture, the dragon oversees rain and flowing water and usually symbolizes happiness and good fortune.* (ForteanPicture Library)

and sowed Drakon's countless teeth in the ground as if planting a crop. To his surprise, full-grown and battle-ready warriors sprang up from each of the seeds, and Drakon's offspring formed a mighty army to serve Cadmus.

The Greek hero Jason also had to battle a drakon to win the legendary Golden Fleece.

SQUIRMS OF THE WORMS

By the year 1000 CE, European lore had cemented the dragon into its favorite folk tales. One of the most famous was the **Lambton worm**, named after a young nobleman of the Northumbria region of England. The young man caught the worm as a small, unidentifiable creature while fishing one day, and threw it down a well. He then went off to fight in the Crusades and returned years later to discover that the throwaway "fish" had grown into a monstrous, reptilian beast large enough to wrap itself around an entire hill—when it wasn't devouring people and livestock.

Lambton ordered an ingenious suit of armor equipped with curving, razor-sharp knives. He taunted the creature to charge him, and then turned so that it landed on the blades. The armor sliced the monster to ribbons and its reign of terror ended.

Another serpent-like dragon of medieval Europe was the **scitalis**. A monster with elegant wings, two clawed front legs, and the lower body of a huge snake, scitalis appeared in several popular bestiaries around 1100-1200 CE. Its two main attributes were excessive body heat, which required it to shed its skin even in mid-winter, and a rainbow skin pattern whose colors had a hypnotic effect on anyone who saw them, to make them easy prey.

The **stollenwurm** (tunnel worm) or **tatzelwurm** (clawed worm) has terrified skiers and hikers in the Swiss Alps since 1789. That year, a pair of tatzelwurms literally scared a man named Hans Fuchs to death. Just before he died of a heart attack caused by the double dragon encounter, he managed to describe to his family what he had seen. One of his relatives created a drawing based on Fuchs' report that continues to fuel tatzelwurm legend to this day.[5]

According to Fuchs, the body and head of the creatures were like those of a lizard, but the face was strangely "catlike."[6] It had a long tail, and its hide was a curious mixture of warts and bristles. The length was about six feet. Sporadic sightings have occurred ever since. In the 1950s a German magazine dispatched a crew to hunt down and photograph the tatzelwurm. The expedition failed, and interest in the creature lessened. A Swiss newspaper reported one of the last known sightings in 1970. A few researchers have maintained that the tatzelwurm is a real creature, perhaps some hardy member of the lizard family.

DRAGON ROOTS

Researchers have long noticed the universality of dragon lore, and many have tried to explain why this monster is so common in world mythology. Both a Munich geology professor and American astronomer Carl Sagan have suggested that an ancient memory—carried in genes inherited from our mammalian ancestors—is responsible for an inborn fear of large reptiles.[7] Prehistoric memories of dinosaurs seep from our subconscious into our impressions of the world, according to this theory, and turn old nightmares into legend.

These fears may have been confirmed in people's minds whenever they accidentally uncovered fossilized dinosaur skeletons, seemingly real proof that such creatures existed.

The Dragon as Drugstore

Although dragons are now considered mythical creatures, certain parts of their carcasses were once in great demand for medicinal purposes. That's assuming, of course, a person could find a dragon body to raid.

The Greek writer Pliny the Elder, who catalogued both known and imaginary animals in his book, *The Natural History*,[8] listed many beneficial uses of dragon parts. Its head brought good fortune when buried under a home's front door, for instance,[9] and its blood was said to heal many diseases. The fat made a salve that could repel venomous snakes. The eyes, if dried, beaten, and mixed with honey, were believed to cure people of nightmares. However, some authorities believe Pliny was actually discussing a species of python, as mentioned earlier in this chapter. Still, the fact that dragons were included in his well-respected encyclopedia of nature convinced many readers of the creatures' reality for centuries.

Some ancient **saurians** still live, however. The **Komodo dragon**, a lizard named after the Indonesian island where Westerners first learned of it in 1912, is the living creature that most closely resembles a traditional dragon. These carnivorous monsters may grow to more than 12 feet in length, and can eat large mammals such as goats. They are related to a fairly recently extinct Australian monitor lizard that could reach three times that length. Although they don't breathe fire or fly, Komodo dragons still present a very formidable appearance and might easily provoke terror-stricken witness reports of dragons if encountered unexpectedly.

Author Peter Costello believes that human craft may have played a role equal to that of nature in reinforcing the idea of dragons. From the early to late Middle Ages, he says in *The Magic Zoo*,[10] the custom of using giant, fluttering windsock dragons as battlefield banners spread from Asia to Europe. Each banner held a flaming torch to present the daunting illusion of a flying, fire-breathing dragon, and may have helped turn the tide of many medieval battles. At night, in the heat of battle, the billowing figures may have appeared real, and those who lived to tell the tale probably swore they battled dragons.

6

Denizens of the Deep

Long ago, when the lakes of North America were new, a guardian was created to sleep below their depths and to keep the sacred waters clean and sparkling. He was named **Misiganebic** and his green, serpent-like body was 30 feet long.

His head was shaped like that of a horse. When the sun shone on his body as he skimmed the surface, his scales glistened in rainbow colors. His beauty was dangerous to behold, however, because anyone who laid eyes on Misiganebic was doomed to die in the very near future.[1] Those who left offerings to him in the lakes he inhabited were always careful to avert their eyes.

Prowling even deeper in the earth and under the biggest bodies of water was **Misikinipik**, a serpent of unimaginable size that was known to the Cree people of Canada. Like his companions and allies, the water lynxes, Misikinipik's head was crowned with great horns.[2]

The water lynx, or **mishipeshu**, known to most indigenous people around the Great Lakes, was shaped like a cat rather than a serpent, with a long tail designed to curl around victims and drag them down into the water. From the horns on its round head to the tip of its tail, the mishipeshu grew a distinctive ridge studded with triangular points.

Water lynxes were known to roil up waves and waterspouts, and often did so while fighting with their eternal airborne enemies, the thunderbirds. Some of the earliest European explorers of the Great Lakes claimed to have glimpsed the water lynx in the 1600s.[3] The

Ojibwe and Menominee believed mishipeshu protected not only the Great Lakes but the sacred copper found on Michigan's Keweenaw Peninsula and Isle Royale.[4]

A rock painting of mishipeshu exists near Lake Superior in Ontario, Canada, along with depictions of several snakes that may represent other water monsters. No one knows how old the paintings are, but those who still tell the tales of these giant beasts hint that they are ancient, indeed.

SEA SNAKES AND THE TROJAN HORSE

Water creatures form a category of monsters that overlaps with many others. There are water-dwelling dragons, chimeras, and the half-humans known as mermen. But lesser-known creatures also paddle and writhe through lake, sea, and stream, according to folklore around the world. Some are beneficial, but most of them do not play well with others.

The Greeks and Romans, as usual, are well represented in the field of mythical sea beasts. Besides the tritons, mermen, sirens, and others already described, there are creatures known as sea snakes. The Roman poet Virgil wrote an epic poem around 20 BCE called *The Aeneid*, about the travels of a Trojan hero named Aeneas.

As Aeneas' hometown of Troy pondered whether to accept a gift of a giant wooden horse offered to them by their enemies, the Greeks, one man named Laocoon decided (correctly) that the horse was a trap and threw his spear at it. Very shortly after that, the citizens of Troy were amazed to see two giant **sea snakes** swimming across the Aegean waters toward the city's harbor. The beasts made straight for Laocoon and immediately slurped him down, and then had his two sons for dessert.

The people of Troy took that incident as an omen that they should accept the horse filled with waiting Greek soldiers, which of course was a huge mistake. So it could be said that the sea snakes had as much to do with the downfall of Troy as did the more famous wooden horse.

The Greeks also told of giant, golden seahorses that pulled the undersea chariots of the god Poseidon. Unlike the tiny creatures we know by that name, these sea horses had the bodies and heads of horses, bronze hooves on their front limbs, but fish tails instead of hind legs. They were also known as hippocamps.

WATER WEIRDIES

Perhaps because undersea life has always been hard for land-based humans to observe, mythical water creatures have been described as some of the strangest of fabulous beasts. One of the weirdest, **Tursus,** comes from Finnish folklore. Its head looks like that of a walrus except for its tall, pointed ears. Its arms and torso appear human, while its hindquarters combine muscular, clawed legs with a fish-like tail. In Finnish legend, Tursus leapt from the ocean at the call of a creator-god, *Wainamoinen*, to help coax the first oak tree to grow from an acorn.[5]

More sinister is **manta**, a monster from the sea off the coast of Chile. Manta is mostly eyes and tentacles, both of which surround its flat, leathery, circular body. On top of the body a cluster of yet more eyes replaces the head, and a clawed tail drifts below. Manta uses its flat body to envelope its victims and hold them in place while it eats them. While the flat body and name are reminiscent of a known creature, the manta ray, the tentacles sound squid-like. According to Chilean folklore, when manta jumps back into the water after basking in the sun, great winds rake the seas.[6]

Another water nasty has the fairytale name of **Nellie Longarms**. Probably the origin of many night terrors in the United Kingdom, Nellie was a bogey-lady of ponds and swamps in several areas of England. English parents warned their children to stay away from water holes or be grabbed by the green, human-like Nellie who would snatch them from below with her long, rubbery arms. Her floating mass of hair, green as pond scum, would muffle the children's cries as they disappeared between her long, emerald teeth.

The fear of Nellie Longarms probably saved many an English child from accidental drowning, and there is a children's book about the legend (*Nellie Longarms Will Get You If You Don't Watch Out*)[7] set in Wybunbury, Chesire. Similar English sea hags are known as Peg Powler and Jenny Greenteeth.

SEA DOGS, SEA HOGS, AND MONK FISH

Off the shores of British Columbia is said to swim a strange aquatic creature known either as the **sea dog** or **sea wolf**. Named mostly for its canine-shaped head, native people of the area have considered it a

Cthulhu: Myth of the Bat-winged Squid God

Some myths are born of modern minds. Horror fiction writer H. P. Lovecraft invented one terrifying sea-beast with the somewhat unpronounceable name of **Cthulhu** (Keh-THOO-loo) in the first half of the twentieth century.

The sea monster Cthulhu lived in a jumble of massive stone ruins somewhere in the Pacific Ocean, and his hideous appearance combined a squid-like, tentacled head with a green, dragon's body and scaled, bat-like wings. Cthulhu's earthly home, wrote Lovecraft in 1928 in "The Call of Cthulhu," lay in the submerged, "nightmare, corpse-like city of R'lyeh, that was built in measureless eons behind history by the vast, loathsome shapes that seeped down from the dark stars. There lay Cthulhu and his hordes . . ."[8]

These vast, loathsome shapes included other huge, alien beings that ranged from fairly pleasant "Elder Gods" to the evil "Great Ones" or "Ancient Ones" like Cthulhu. The creatures inhabited earth in its early, formative years, when the strange "star-spawn" built giant stone cities that now lie in ruins in the unexplored corners of the earth.

totem or tribal animal for hundreds of years. The creature swims with flipper-like limbs, is sometimes seen with tusks and wings, and has a long and sinuous body. Some authorities speculate these creatures may actually be leopard seals, a type of Antarctic seal with a spotted throat, long neck, and reptilian-shaped head. Leopard seals may grow up to 10 feet in length and may behave very aggressively.

Sea dogs also show up on many European coats of arms. While the sea dog's body looks canine, scales rather than fur cover its skin. The European sea dog is also built to swim with webbed feet, ears and tail, and a serrated, fish-like fin down the center of its back.

Lovecraft returned to his uneasy universe over and over in a group of stories written between 1928 and 1936. His fantasy world was so compelling that other writers such as Robert Bloch, Colin Wilson, and Lovecraft's publisher August Derleth wrote their own stories based on what Derleth called "the Cthulhu Mythos," a fictional mythology with its own gods, cities, and even ancient texts.

The Necronomicon, an imaginary book Lovecraft referred to and quoted in some of his tales, has taken on a life of its own. Supposedly written by a worshipper of Cthulhu with instructions on summoning "The Old Ones," Lovecraft's invented codex has appeared outside his tales in hoaxed library catalogs and in full, fictional books purporting to be the original *Necronomicon*.

Although Lovecraft never intended his stories to be read as other than fiction, author Joyce Carol Oates says in a preface to one collection of his tales that some Lovecraft fans believe Cthulhu to be entirely real. They argue, Oates said, "that . . . Lovecraft was in fact transcribing history, or prehistory."[9] Whether or not Cthulhu's fan base accepts him as ancient reality, Cthulhu enthusiasts support a wide range of tentacled Cthulhu merchandise from T-shirts to cuddly, plush Cthulhu dolls.

Figure 6.1 *Cthulhu, a sea monster with tentacles on its head, a dragon-like body, and wings, first appeared in the work of horror-fiction writer H. P. Lovecraft in 1928.* (Linda S. Godfrey)

European sailors from around 1500 CE began describing **sea hogs**, creatures with the tail of a fish but the front legs, head, and tusks of a hog. Later, the name referred to porpoises taken at sea for their meat.

The thirteenth through sixteenth centuries were also a time when sailors from Denmark to China reported sightings of a strange, human-shaped, and human-headed creature with scaled flippers and tail, and a torso that resembled the cape of a monk. Its hairstyle, shaven on the crown and the rest cut chin length, was also like those sported by some monastic orders. Altogether, its humble appearance earned it the title of **monkfish**. Modern science considers these early descriptions of monkfish to be fanciful legend, as they bear little resemblance to the large-mouthed, bottom dwelling species known to modern science as the monkfish.

Mothers of All Monsters

For many ancient cultures, the original sources of life on earth were massive ocean monsters big enough to encircle the world. Perhaps early people connected the saltwater of the oceans with their own salty-tasting blood and water-filled wombs. It may also have been that the sea and its foaming waves seemed like an immense, animated force, a serpent as large as the whole world.

The Indian **Sesha** (or **Shesha**) is one of the oldest examples of "world serpents." Sometimes called **Ananta Sesha**, this water beast had as many as one thousand heads that, when they yawned, created earthquakes. Sesha lay in a stack of its own coils on the ocean floor and acted as a bed for the god Vishnu whenever he wanted to sleep. According to Hindu mythology, Sesha will play his final role at the end of the world, when each of his heads will spit poison.

Norse mythology's world serpent, **Jormungand**, was also called the Midgard Serpent. Jormungand was born so hideous that his parents, the trickster god Loki and the giant frost goddess Angrboda, threw him into the sea. Loose in the unbounded waters, Jormungand gobbled up fish until he grew large enough to encircle the world. Like Sesha, Jormungand is also expected to play a role in the end of the world when he at last thrusts his rainbow coils out of the water to unleash his venom upon humanity. Then he will wage his final and mutually fatal battle with Thor, god of thunder.

Moshiriikkwechep is the name of the vast, world-back trout of Japan. Pictured as a giant fish rather than serpent, Moshiriikkwechep is so large that its every movement can cause earthquakes or storms, so it is kept buried in ocean mud by other gods most of the time. The creature was designed to carry the world on its spine.

Mythology from the region of the Pacific island of Fiji included several large serpent gods. One of the most interesting, **Ratu Mai Bulu,** could create islands by raising the ocean floor. He represented fertility and growth, and punished offenders by covering them with writhing snakes.

Two Heads Are Creepier than One: Beings with Numerous Noggins

In the mythic days of the ancient Greeks, it took extremely fearsome monsters to guard treasures or castle gates from invading heroes sent by the gods. A simple dog, no matter how large, could never do the job.

So when the gods needed a guardian of the underworld, they sent a dog with three heads (some stories say up to 100), each one crawling with snakes. His name was Cerberus, and he was one of a handful of hideous children born to the half-serpent woman Echidne and the multi-dragon-headed Typhon.

While Cerberus allowed most dead people to pass into Hades, his barking, biting heads efficiently stopped any living visitors or would-be escapees. Greek heroes, however, have a way of overcoming monstrous obstacles, and no fewer than three of them connived a way past the yapping menace.

Aeneas, hero of Troy, wanted to get into the underworld to consult with his dead father on some matters. The Sibyl, a long-lived prophetess, helped Aeneas by advising him to drug Cerberus with a mixture of honey and herbal opiates. The ploy worked, and Aeneas was able to wander freely in Hades.

Another hero, Orpheus, had a search-and-rescue operation in mind for his visit to Hades. His wife had recently died from a snakebite, and he wanted her back. Orpheus possessed a magical talent for music; both his voice and his playing of the lyre, or small harp, were said to enchant all living creatures. He used this skill to lull Cerberus to sleep, and then he slipped through the gate while the three heads all nodded off.

The third hero to try his luck with the three-headed canine was Heracles (or Hercules, to the Romans). He had been commanded by the gods to descend to the underworld and fetch Cerberus, without use of any sort of weapon. Heracles, known for his great strength, didn't bother with trickery like music or drugs. Instead, he used his powerful hands to get a stranglehold on all three of Cerberus' necks and wrestle the great beast into submission. He triumphantly dragged Cerberus back to earth and presented him to the gods, but the morning sun awoke the mega-mutt. Cerberus managed to hightail it back to Hades, and he has guarded the underworld's gate ever since.

MEDUSA; WHEN LOOKS COULD KILL

Fans of the fictional series *Harry Potter* will recognize Cerberus in J.K. Rowling's three-headed guardian of the sorcerer's stone, Fluffy.[1] Rowling followed the trail blazed by the Greek tale in giving Fluffy a weakness for music, and added a comic element with massive amounts of dog drool. But most polycephalic creatures are not so easily tamed.

One of the most famous was Medusa, one of the three sisters known as **Gorgons,** huge women with hog's teeth and long, brass claws. Medusa is famous for her dreadlock-like hairdo composed of snakes rather than braids. Although Medusa actually possessed only one human head, the addition of the snakes gave her the appearance of a multiheaded creature.

At one time, according to the legend, Medusa was a beautiful human female who was very proud of her long, shining tresses. Her fatal mistake lay in daring to compare herself to the goddess, Minerva, who didn't enjoy being challenged by a mortal. Minerva gave the maiden a

Figure 7.1   *Cerberus, a ferocious dog with three heads, guarded the entrance to Hades, the Greek underworld.* (Nathan Godfrey)

monstrous makeover, and changed her silky hair into a nest of writhing serpents.

Medusa's extreme ugliness immediately turned anyone who saw her into stone, and the land where she lived became filled with what looked like statues of the men, women, children, and animals who had mistakenly set eyes upon her.

The hero Perseus eventually killed Medusa after he cleverly used his metal shield as a mirror. He was then able to sneak up on the horrendous hag without looking directly at her, and cut off her head as a prize for Minerva.

SCYLLA, A ONE-WOMAN SEXTET

Scylla was another female Greek monster that began life as a beauty. She was one of the loveliest of the sea nymphs, and several of the gods fell in love with her. That did not set well with the goddess Circe, who decided to make Scylla less attractive. Circe filled the sea around Scylla with a special poison, and the nymph suddenly found herself surrounded by six yowling, dog-like heads . . . all attached to her waist. Each head had a pair of canine legs, which also sprouted from Scylla's torso. Forced into a cave in the Straits of Messina, she survived by clawing at passing ships and devouring everyone aboard. Eventually, she was turned into a rock that became famous for causing shipwrecks.

THE HYDRA: HEADS WITH DOUBLE THE FUN

Like his brother Cerberus, the **Hydra** also inherited the ability to grow more than one head from their father, Typhon. But while Cerberus was canine in form, the Hydra was all snake—or more accurately, all snakes. The exact number of serpent heads carried on the Hydra's scaly shoulders ranges from seven to 1,000, depending on the source. But all of them exhaled poisonous fumes. Trying to decapitate the Hydra was a classic exercise in futility, since whenever one head was chopped off, two more would grow in its place. And one special head was immortal and could not be killed by any means.

The hero Heracles, who would later drag Cerberus from the underworld, was also given the task of slaying the Hydra. Heracles quickly learned that he would have to do more than slash at the heads. He finally discovered that if he burned the flesh of each neck as soon as its head was severed, it couldn't grow back. In this way, he cleared the monster of all heads except the invincible one. Since he could do nothing to that head, he attacked the body instead, slicing it away from the head, which he then buried deep in the earth. With no way to dig itself out, the last Hydra head would lie awake in its grave for all eternity.

CACUS, THE ORIGINAL SPIDER MAN

Cacus, a giant spider-like creature whose name meant "wicked," was yet another monster done in by Heracles. Although its huge body was like that of a house-sized spider, three human heads rode atop its dome-like torso on one long neck. Its legs were no spindly arthropod's but grew thick like an elephant's to more efficiently stomp its enemies to death.

The spider-monster's mother was Medusa, and his father was Vulcan, god of fire. As a result, his three heads could all shoot flames from their mouths. This made Cacus very dangerous to approach.

Cacus hid out in a cave when he wasn't out laying waste to the countryside and eating everyone's cattle and relatives. He sealed his doom, however, when he stole some cattle from Heracles as the hero was passing through the area. Although he tried his best to ward off the enraged Heracles with great clouds of fire, Heracles managed to grab him by his slender neck and tie it into a knot. This put the three heads in a mangled, twisted position so that they could no longer work together or shoot flames without burning one another, and after a while they all choked to death. Cacus' body made a great feast for every bird of prey.

A MANY-HEADED MISCELLANY

The Yakut people of Siberia live in a region of mountains and tundra, with brutally long and cold winters. In their folk belief a two-headed

Double Dragon: Real Creatures with Two Heads

More dragons boast multiheads than any other legendary creature. Two-headed (**bicephalic**) and other multiheaded (**polycephalic**) dragons are almost a cliché in fairy tales and mythology. But a California couple named Frank and Barbarba Witte were astounded in June 2007, when one of their pet bearded dragons, reptiles native to Australia, produced a two-headed offspring. Named Zak-n-Wheezie after a two-headed cartoon dragon in the Columbia Pictures series *Dragon Tales*, each head is fed slightly mashed Pakistani cockroaches to keep the whole critter healthy.[2]

Although bearded dragons may live 10 years and reach a length of about two feet, Zak-n-Wheezie made the Guinness World Records in 2008 when it reached its first birthday as the longest-lived bicephalic bearded dragon known. And although two-headed lizards are rare, another was hatched to bearded dragon breeders William and Jan Davis in Kernersville, North Carolina, in early April 2008.

Other reptiles have also doubled their brainpower. In 2006 a man from the Chinese city of Qingdao found a two-headed golden coin turtle at an animal market.[3]

Most of these creatures are actually created in the same way as conjoined twins, formed when two embryos partially merge early in their development. Each head will usually have its own brain, and the heads share control of the body and organs, which can make movement difficult. Some two-headed snakes have even been observed trying to swallow one another.

eagle named **ai tojon** nests in the top branches of the giant tree that represents the world. He is the creator of light.

In New Guinea, the Arapesh people believe that striped snakes with two heads inhabit their ponds. The monstrous creatures guard sacred hunting grounds and are a lesser type of spirit beings known as **walinab**.[4]

The Sioux Indians of the North American plains tell stories of a very hirsute giant with two faces and large, elephant-like ears that can digest human victims. **Two Faces**, as the creature is known, reproduces by turning humans into juvenile versions of itself.[5]

Aillen Trechenn, which means "triple-headed," was the name of a three-headed monster that terrorized County Roscommon in Ireland. It lived near an ancient burial mound, and was most likely to attack humans on the Celtic holiday we now know as Halloween.[6]

Creatures to Look Up To: The Giants

Witiko tasted the strong north wind, stretched forth one of his long, hoary arms, and wound his jagged claws around the trunk of the tallest pine tree. Snow flew in great swaths from the tree's branches as Witiko wrenched it from the frozen ground, and then uprooted the next tallest pine. Laying the fallen trees on the hard-packed snow, he slipped a narrow, taloned foot between the branches of each and began to glide on them as if they were snowshoes. His hunger burned fierce within the hollow that served as his stomach, and only human flesh would give him some momentary relief.

He strode until he came upon the moccasin tracks of two men. They would be hunters, he knew, looking for meat for their family's stewpot, but Witiko did not fear their arrows. His white fur was thick, and his heart of ice could break any stone tip. The white star on his forehead blazed brighter as he neared them, his massive stride covering many times the distance of a human step.

When at last he sighted the buckskin clothing of the two hunters dark against the snow, he could not help letting forth an ear-splitting roar, so loud that a snowslide rumbled down a nearby mountain at the sound. The hunters turned, and their eyes grew wide in fear. One began to glide away on his own, expertly crafted snowshoes, but the other was so frightened that he crouched in the snow. Witiko stopped for a moment, unsure what the man was going to do.

The hunter's body had reacted to his fear by making him relieve his bowels, and the panicked man then threw his excrement at Witiko. Witiko became so confused by this that he paused just long enough for the hunter to get back on his feet and scramble into a nearby cave in a rock cleft too narrow for Witiko to follow.

Witiko turned his attention to the other hunter and caught up with him in two strides, bringing one pine tree snowshoe down on the hunter to kill him in a single stroke. Now he would have a meal.

When he had devoured the hunter, he took the skull and hung it on a necklace made from the sinews of an elk. The necklace already hung heavy with the skulls of other victims. He turned to leave, but wrinkled his great nose in irritation at the smell of smoke. There stood the first hunter, and this time his arm was drawn back and ready to release an arrow that burned with fire the hunter had kindled in the cave. Before Witiko could move, the hunter let the arrow fly and it sank deep into the monster's giant ice heart.

Witiko clutched his chest and pulled the arrow out, but it was too late. His heart had begun to melt, and the fire was spreading to his icy bones. He shrank and shrank until only the core of his ice heart remained, and finally it, too, dissolved to reveal a dead and very wrinkled old man.

This, the hunter knew, was a man who had wandered into the forest years ago and had never been seen again. A tribe of Witikos had adopted the lost one, it was whispered, and changed him into one of them. The hunter could see now that the whispers were true. He then looked with sorrow at the skull that had belonged to his hunting companion. Shouldering the great necklace made of the Witiko's trophies so that he could take them to be properly buried, he trudged back to his village to deliver his bittersweet news.

The witiko, or **windigo**, is a prominent monster in the lore of North American native peoples from Wisconsin to Canada. There are many variations on the tale, but the cannibalistic ice giant that stood taller than the trees is one of the most common visions of the monster. The creature could be defeated by magic or by melting its ice to reveal a lost human in its heart, but one other known defense was to fling excrement at the monster to blind and confuse it.[1]

OVERSIZED ANCIENTS

Almost every known culture includes larger-than-life-sized villains and heroes in its legend and lore. And some anthropologists believe that creatures such as Witiko were based on memories of actual super-sized people, whose recovered bones show that giants have indeed walked the earth. Of course, there is always the question of how tall a person must be to qualify as a giant. But many skeletons that predate Columbus' exploration and that measure over seven feet tall have been discovered around the United States.

One burial mound near Charleston, West Virginia, contained an individual who once stood seven-foot-six and may have belonged to a culture now termed the Adena. The Adena people flourished between 1000 BCE and 200 CE[2] and probably did seem like giants to the other, shorter indigenous groups of the time. But these days, people seven to seven-and-one-half feet tall are simply considered examples of extreme height, and may be paid big bucks to play basketball.

Antwerp's Anti-Twerp

Europeans tell their own tales of giants from days gone by. In Antwerp, Belgium, the most authoritative voices of the day reported around 1500 CE that the bones of a giant named **Druon Antigoon** lay in a stone castle in that town. Artist Albrecht Durer, known for his meticulously realistic drawings of people and animals, viewed the bones and estimated they belonged to a man who stood 18 feet tall. Historic Antwerp legends remembered Druon Antigoon as a massive oaf who camped by the Scheldt River and demanded payment from all those who crossed. Antigoon chopped the right hands from anyone who failed to pay. A brave general in Julius Caesar's army finally beheaded the terrifying giant.

The problem with the Antigoon legend is that the bones were eventually proved to be those of a whale, not a human.[3] Giant legends die hard, however, especially since they are found in so many ancient sources that seem to support their existence. The Book of Genesis in the Hebrew Bible hints at giants in chapter six, speaking of the days of Noah, "the **Nephilim** were on the earth in those days—and also afterward—when the sons of God went to the daughters of men and had children by them. They were the heroes of old, men of renown."[4]

Giants of the Bible

Nephilim has often been taken to mean "giants," but it actually means "fallen ones" in Hebrew. It did also denote very large and robust people, however, because in Numbers 13, the Nephilim are described as so big that the Israelites felt like grasshoppers next to them.

According to some Hebrew texts, the great Israelite leader Moses mentioned at least one giant, **Palet**,[5] also known as **Og**, as having survived the flood because he was either too tall to drown or was able to hitch a ride on the roof of the ark. He eventually battled Moses using a mountain as a weapon, but was defeated—or de-feeted—when Moses chopped off his feet with a massive ax.[6] Og is also referred to as the King of Bashan in the Book of Joshua. Various legends put Og's height anywhere from nine feet to a few miles high.

One of the most famous giants of all time is the biblical **Goliath**, a Philistine army champion who stood over nine feet tall and carried a spear as thick as a weaver's rod. Goliath lost his big head, of course, to the young and comparatively small David, who flung a stone into Goliath's forehead before the giant could manage to draw back his spear. (Slingshots used in battle were "somewhat larger than a baseball . . . hurled by a master slinger, they probably traveled at close to 100 miles per hour.")[7]

More clues to the nature of ancient giants may be found in the root of our word, giant, which comes from a Sanskrit phrase that

Figure 8.1 *David (right) and Goliath (left) prepare to do battle. David defeat-ed the giant Goliath by using a slingshot to propel a rock into Goliath's forehead before he had a chance to use his spear.* (Time & Life Pictures/ Getty Images)

meant "earth" and "giant."[8] Most creation myths include some type of monstrous being that either arises from the earth or gives of itself to become the earth.

Giants of World Creation

The Aztecs believed that the substance of the earth came from a female giant named **Tlaltecuhtli**, who was large enough to ride the ocean as if she sat upon a horse. She was human-like in appearance, except for having great fangs rather than teeth and extra mouths on every joint

Gigantism: Too Much of a Good Thing

They are not ogres, not primordial titans of creation, and certainly not gods, but human beings who suffer from a condition known as **gigantism** nevertheless tower over most other people. One of the earliest on record with reasonably reliable measurements, Englishman John Middleton, was born in 1578. Also known as the "Childe of Hale," he measured nine feet, three inches tall and his hands were 17 inches long.

In gigantism the bones are over-fueled by too much growth hormone, a substance secreted by the pituitary gland, until they surpass normal measurements. It's generally not a healthy condition. People with gigantism may have much shorter life spans—John Middleton died at the age of 45—and suffer from other symptoms such as thickened facial bones, headaches, vision problems, and disproportionately large feet and hands. When diagnosed early, the condition can often be arrested via surgery on the pituitary gland.

Because gigantism is a very rare condition, those who have it often become famous. Giant people were once in demand by the crown heads of Europe for their sensational looks and because they made imposing courtiers and guards. Three brothers all around eight feet tall once guarded the Tower of London, and Queen Elizabeth employed a porter who stood over seven and one-half feet tall.[9]

Another set of giant brothers ranging from seven and one-half feet to nearly eight feet tall were born in Texas in the mid-1800s and appeared of her body. The gods Quetzalcoatl and Tezcatlipoca ripped her in two to create the earth and the sky.[10]

P'an Ku was the gigantic man-god of the Chinese who named the sky and earth and whose body became their five holy mountains. **Rigi,** a giant of Micronesian legend, was so tall that back when the earth and

with the Barnum and Bailey Circus in the late 1880s. Billed as "The Tallest Men on Earth," advertisements promised a reward of $100 to anyone who could stand on the same ground as the brothers and reach a dollar bill they held over their heads.

One of the most famous ultra-tall people in the United States was Robert Wadlow of Alton, Illinois, born in 1918 and called the Gentle Giant for his soft-spoken ways. Wadlow stood six feet tall by age eight, and ended up at a whopping eight feet, eleven and one-half inches in height by his early twenties.

His parents refused pituitary treatment for him. Wadlow attended public schools and joined the Boy Scouts in pursuit of a normal life. But the weakness of his bones, an unfortunate side effect of gigantism, restricted his activity. Also, most objects that others take for granted such as furniture, writing implements, and even shoes and clothing were impossibly small for his use. Since this made going away to college very difficult, he accepted a job promoting shoes with the company that made his custom oxfords, and later appeared as a main big-tent attraction with the Ringling Brothers and Barnum and Bailey Circus.

Wadlow died of a leg infection in 1940, partly because his long limbs had so little feeling in them that he didn't notice a sore in time to treat it. A bronze, life-sized statue of the Gentle Giant and a replica of the giant, custom chair he sat in stand in a park in Alton in memory of the town's most memorable citizen.

the sky were still mashed together, he was given the job of separating them and setting the sky up where it belonged. His upper body then formed the Milky Way, and his legs sank down into the ground and became the source of all earthworms.

According to Norse mythology, the ice giant **Ymir**'s body provided raw materials for the earth,[11] and the fire giant, **Muspel** or **Surt**, was associated with the end of the world as it gave of its flame to burn all living things. The Babylonian giantess, Tiamat, was also split in two to become both heaven and earth.

A more unusual legend comes from the Mesopotamian people known as the Hittites. The Hittite giant **Upelluri** lived in the middle of the sea, where he stood not quite tall enough to reach the surface. The god Kumarbi used him as a supportive stand upon which to grow his son **Ullikummi,** who grew into a giant made of diorite stone.

There are other numerous examples of ancient mythic giants, and the Greeks and Romans, as usual, provide a slew of them.

Freaks of the Greeks

The **Titans** were the original massive beings of the Greeks, birthed from a mating of the sky and the earth. They became the first generation of gods, who ruled until defeated by Zeus and others of the second generation. But Zeus and his crew later had to fight against the **giants**, huge beings that looked human except for their snake tails. Zeus managed to defeat them by siring Heracles (Hercules), the half-divine hero who did indeed kill them all off.

The **Cyclopes** (that's a plural) were one-eyed gigantic beings that helped Zeus by making thunder and lightning for him. There were at least three Cyclopes; some tales suggest there were others. **Polyphemus** became one of the best-known Cyclopes because of his battle with the hero Odysseus, who robbed Polyphemus of his one eye so that he and his men could escape the giant's cave.

Talos was another famous Greek giant. Made of bronze, he guarded the island of Crete by heating his metallic body until it glowed, then

Figure 8.2 *Robert Wadlow of Alton, Illinois, was almost 9 feet tall by his early 20s.* (Bettmann/Corbis)

hugging invaders until they burned to a crisp. His weakness was that he had one vein in his body, and the Gorgon Medusa managed to slice his ankle so that his blood all rushed out, killing him.

Perhaps the most famous Greek giant of all, however, was **Atlas,** whose shoulders were broad enough to hold up the heavens. He was able to trick the hero Heracles into taking over for him for a short time, but was in turn outsmarted by the hero and ended up eternally shouldering the sky.

MORE HUMONGOUS HUMANITY

Giants of medieval times are almost too numerous to mention. Often depicted as **ogres**—ugly, misshapen, and cannibalistic monsters— they survive in children's fairy tales such as *Jack and the Beanstalk* with its ogre at the top of the beanstalk, screaming for the blood of an Englishman.

Many of these tales crossed the ocean with European emigrants and mutated into American myths such as **Paul Bunyan**, legendary logger of Midwestern lumber camps. Bunyan, with his giant blue ox, Babe, was a kindly giant rather than an ogre. As a newborn, he was so large that five storks had to carry him to his parents. He used a pine tree as a hairbrush, and his frying pan was so large that it had to be greased by four men skating around it with hog fat tied onto their boots. When a twisting river irritated him because it was hard for log barges to navigate its tight turns, he fashioned a giant chain and pulled the river straight.

Another American giant turned out to be more mischief than myth. In 1869 several well-diggers working on a farm in Cardiff, New York, uncovered what appeared to be a petrified (hardened to stone), 10-foot man.[12] The **Cardiff giant**, as he came to be known, turned out to be the work of an atheist named George Hull who wished to poke fun at the idea of biblical giants. Hull commissioned a stonecutter to carve the figure, then plotted with the owner of the farm. He planned to expose his own hoax after letting religious leaders claim it as proof that giants once existed.

The hoaxed figure became such a popular attraction that showman P.T. Barnum built his own replica, which is now on display at Marvin's Marvelous Mechanical Museum outside of Detroit, Michigan. The original stone statue is in the Farmer's Museum in Cooperstown, New York.

Dealers in Death: Werewolves, Hellhounds, and Vampires

Humans have always connected dogs and wolves with death, graveyards, and the underworld. Find a boneyard and some sort of canine will likely lurk nearby—either to guard or to scavenge. In ancient times, the mythic, three-headed Cerberus guarded the gates of Hades for the Greeks, and Anubis, the jackal-headed god of the Egyptian underworld, served as "god of the cemetery."[1] But one type of otherworldly dog seems to have survived to present times.

The **hellhound**, a black, phantom creature with glowing red eyes, appears at times of death and distress in macabre stories from around the world. Stories of hellhounds are particularly common in the British Isles where it is also known as **Black Shuck**, the **gyrtrash** and other names. These phantoms have terrorized England's churchyards and crossroads for centuries.

But hellhounds are by no means tethered to northern Europe. A California man who prefers to be identified only as John claims three encounters with hellhounds. Each incident occurred at a time when his life was in jeopardy.

One night in late December of 2002, John and his girlfriend were sitting in the living room of his home in a town, which he noted, was built over a Chumash Native American burial ground. The couple was watching TV when suddenly they both felt a strong urge to look at the front window. Staring back at them was a black dog with red, glowing eyes. It stood at least five feet tall on all fours, and John noticed that although its muzzle was right next to the glass, the window did not fog. The dog's appearance was "ethereal," said John, yet he and his girlfriend both saw it clearly.

John estimated that they gazed at it in shock for 15-20 seconds before he gathered his wits and jumped off the sofa to fling open the door. But there was no dog—or any other creature—in sight. A few days after the dog's appearance, John was almost killed in a car crash that wrecked his 1987 Caprice Classic station wagon. But it would take two other incidents before John began to connect the dog with dire moments in his life.

The next year, in 2003, John was put on a pain medication for a chronic medical condition. He suffered an adverse reaction to the drug, and was rushed to the emergency room by ambulance. On the way, he happened to look out the vehicle's rear window and was stunned to see the same black dog staring at him with those glowing red eyes! As it turned out, he nearly died before doctors were able to treat the reaction.

Incredibly, the Black Shuck would make one more appearance. In 2004 John suffered yet another life-threatening reaction to medication for the same ailment, and this time, he was pronounced clinically dead for over two minutes. The last thing he saw before his heart stopped was the huge black hound, standing next to his hospital bed, its red eyes boring into John's as he lost consciousness.

John was never sure whether the creature's visits were intended to usher him into the next life, to warn him of danger, or if the dog simply came to observe like some type of spiritual vulture. In any case, he hopes never to see it again.

BLACK SHUCK AND OTHER PHANTOM DOGS

John was not exactly comforted to learn that many others have witnessed similar black dogs. One of Great Britain's most famous spectral hounds, Black Shuck, has been seen near Norfolk since the early 1840s and its description matches that of the creature in John's California sightings. The size of a calf, with black fur and red eyes, the British animal is said to portend death—or at least, very bad luck—for anyone who sees it. A variation near Leicestershire is called the **Black Shug**. Both "Shuck" and "Shug" may be derived from the Anglo-Saxon word, *soucca*, which means Satan.

Another British Isles harbinger of death is the **Black Dog of Ardura**, which has appeared on the island of Mull in the Inner Hebrides since the early 1900s. Witnesses included several family doctors who observed it lurking nearby the homes of patients about to die. According to author Patricia Dale-Green, sightings of this sort of phantom dog are reported all over Europe, especially near public byways, religious sites, and bodies of water.[2]

In northern Europe—Scandinavia, Denmark, and Germany—giant phantom dogs are usually black poodles! Their glowing red eyes reveal their demonic nature. Patricia Dale-Green's *Lore of the Dog* tells the tale of a Dane on horseback who was attacked by a black, phantom poodle while riding at night. The poodle jumped atop the horse from the rear and began to grow in weight. The horse stumbled and faltered under the increasing passenger load and its legs had almost buckled from the pressure when the man reached home and the phantom dog sprang away.[3]

The black dog phenomenon occurs in South America, too. Argentine sugar mills, according to folk beliefs, are guarded at night by red-eyed, black ghost dogs that do the bidding of the mills' devilish owners and—whether real or not—serve as efficient theft prevention.

WEREWOLVES: GOING BERSERK

Black phantom dogs may be related to another legendary canine, the **werewolf**. The main difference between the two is that the traditional werewolf is primarily a human that has either transformed his flesh or projected his spirit-body double into the shape of a wolf, while phantom black dogs are ghost-like but not at all human in nature.

While earlier chapters have shown that the concept of human-animal combinations is ancient and widespread, many historians trace the modern concept of werewolves back to Scandinavian warriors known as **berserkers**. These warriors would wear bear or wolf skins into battle, often howling like beasts and even biting their shields to appear like ferocious animals.

Some Norse legends claimed that the men actually transformed themselves into werewolves and werebears. This undoubtedly contributed to the berserkers' ability to terrify their enemies. The stories lingered long after the battles had ended and spread widely, cementing the connection between animal skins and magical transformation throughout Europe.

A Finnish folktale, for instance, tells of a Finn who used either the afterbirth (placenta) or the fur of a wolf to transform, simply by pulling the wolf remains over his head. Folklorist Knut Strompdal collected one such story in 1939 from a Norwegian farmer who said a friend had shown him his magic wolf skin and offered to let him try it. The farmer declined, afraid that he might commit mayhem under the skin's influence.[4]

Ways of the Werewolf

The werewolf has evolved from simple folk tales to a complex modern mythology aided and abetted by Hollywood movies. Thanks largely to the *Wolfman* film series starring Lon Chaney, Jr., current folk belief dictates werewolves are created by a bite from another werewolf. They live most of the time as humans, but transform bodily and go on murderous rampages on nights when the moon is full. They can be resisted by holy water, crosses, and wolfsbane, but must be killed by a silver bullet. Once mortally wounded, the beast will revert to human form before death.

A surprising number of contemporary people believe they are werewolves and call themselves **lycanthropes**, or **lycans**. They claim that they transform into wolves under the full moon, in body, spirit or both. Lycan Web sites feature forum discussions on topics ranging from transformation experiences to planned social events . . . often set in nature areas.

While modern lycans claim the human-wolf transition is possible, they have yet to prove their magical transformations to the rest of the world. However, creatures resembling the stereotypical werewolf are occasionally sighted in present times.

The Beast of Bray Road . . . and Elsewhere

Hundreds of witnesses around the United States and other countries have reported seeing a wolf-headed, fully canine creature that walks upright and threatens or chases people but doesn't physically attack anyone. Some sightings are in broad daylight, and incidents seem unconnected to the full moon.

While the phenomenon is widespread, the states of Wisconsin and Michigan are particular sighting hotbeds. (This author has chronicled many reports and theories in *The Beast of Bray Road, Tailing Wisconsin's Werewolf,*[5] and *Hunting the American Werewolf.*[6]) The creature was nicknamed **The Beast of Bray Road** in a December 31, 1991, newspaper story because many of the first publicly reported sightings occurred outside of Elkhorn, Wisconsin, in the vicinity of a country lane by that name.

In these reports, some supernatural elements are occasionally present such as human-like behavior, impressions of telepathic messages from the creatures, or even a glimpse of the creature partially "morphing" or transforming. However, most of the incidents describe a wolf-like animal that is unusual only in its behavior: walking or running upright and sometimes eating or carrying prey with its forelimbs.

The author also believes it is possible these reports describe some little understood adaptation of natural wolves that has been misinterpreted through the ages and thereby brought about the idea of werewolves. And yet, it's hard to imagine such a large mammal remaining mostly undetected in areas of dense human population.

Many indigenous traditions claim the creature is an ancient spirit being that comes and goes. Until one is captured, however, every guess as to its true nature—human werewolf, natural species adapted to walk upright, or spirit creature—is as good as another.

BLOODSUCKERS

Where werewolves tread, it seems, **vampires** also flap. Vampires are similar to other archetypal monsters in that almost every culture contains some tradition of a creature that sneakily drains people of their blood, life force, or even emotions. And vampires have followed werewolves as the inspiration of a modern mythos created by popular literature and film.

In 1819 a British doctor named John Polidori wrote ***The Vampyre***, a short novel based on a story he had heard from one of his patients, the famous writer Lord Byron. Its success was followed by a novel published in 1847, *Varney the Vampire; or The Feast of Blood*. Although composed of shorter serials probably written by several authors in 220 episodes, research has shown the main *Varney* author was James Malcolm Rymer of Scotland.

Irish writer Bram Stoker's 1897 novel ***Dracula*** continued to hone the image of the cultured, antiheroic vampire that had already been set in the two earlier works. Since that time, fantasy authors galore and a slew of Hollywood movies have completed the creature's transformation into the caped, urbane creature of the night that permeates modern media.

Contemporary vampire basics are well known. The modern vampire sleeps in a coffin by day and drains people of their blood at night in order to avoid injurious sunlight. New vampires are "sired" by the bite of an established vampire. Garlic, holy water, and crosses protect people against the flying ghouls, and a vampire has no reflection in a mirror. A vampire is virtually immortal unless it is staked through the heart with a sturdy piece of wood, preferably white thorn aspen or a shard of the creature's own coffin, and can take the form of a bat to travel or get in and out of tight places.

The Female of the Species

Not all vampires are male, of course. Legends of female undead who rose at night to drink the blood of innocent youngsters date back to Old Testament times in the Middle East. A creature named **Lilith**, who was the first wife of Adam according to Hebrew lore, turned to vampirism to attack Adam's children with Eve. And Greek parents feared **Lamia**, a goddess who became a child-hunting, demonic vampire after Hera, her competitor for the affections of the god Zeus, killed Lamia's children.

The label of vampire has sometimes been applied to people even when there was little evidence to justify it. One incident occurred in Foster, Rhode Island, in the early 1800s when Nancy Young, the 19-year-old daughter of a sea captain, became sick and died, perhaps of tuberculosis. Before she died, her sister and a handful of other young people also contracted Nancy's malady. It was somehow decided that Nancy was a vampire, and her body was dug up and burned. The sick children were made to inhale the smoke from her corpse in hopes that they would be cured, and Nancy became forever known as the **Vampire of Foster**.[7]

Ghouls Go Global

Humanity has invented an endless variety vampires, each ethnic group creating its own unique undead. One of the weirdest was a Croatian vampire tale from the coastal island of Lastovo in the late 1730s that involved court testimony claiming vampires caused plague and diarrhea. A citizen group armed themselves with stakes made of black thorn, and began hunting vampires by opening graves to look for corpses that had not decayed.

Local legend had it that at least one grave contained a vampire that tried to run away but was shot by a priest. Any corpses that appeared too fresh for the length of time they had been buried were staked and otherwise mutilated. Eventually, the vampire hunts stopped after 17 participants were found guilty of desecrating graves.[8]

In the Philippines, people shudder at the **aswang**, one of the world's most bizarre vampires. It appears either as a head with no body or a very old woman, and possesses the power of flight. The aswang's main prey is the unborn child, which it sucks from pregnant women's bellies with an ultra-long tongue. The aswang was the subject of a self-titled 1993 movie made by Aswang Productions.

Challenge of the Chupacabras

Another fast-growing body of mythology has wrapped itself around the entity known as the **chupacabras**, or "goat-sucker," reported all over the Americas but particularly in Puerto Rico. Like a traditional vampire, it drains its victims, usually domestic animals, of blood, but its appearance is humanoid rather than human.

Most eyewitnesses describe it as a grayish, bat-winged creature able to stand upright on muscular hind legs, and measuring three to five feet in height. Its puny front limbs end in three-clawed "hands," and its eyes are large and red. Glistening, iridescent spines run down its back and its sharp teeth can cleanly remove body parts or puncture skin for blood removal.

Although the vampiric creature was whispered about in Puerto Rican folklore over the last several decades of the twentieth century, it first came to worldwide attention in 1995 when villagers began complaining that they were losing pets and livestock to the beast's depredations. One eyewitness, Madelyne Maldonado, looked out her window one day to see a four-foot, dark-gray creature with feathery "frills" on its back approaching a cat that was slowly backing away from it.[9]

Figure 9.1   *The chupacabras is known throughout the Americas, especially Puerto Rico, for killing and draining the blood of pets and livestock.* (Troy Therrien)

Noble Nightmares

Despite the grisly nature of all vampire stories, the vampire has been strangely co-opted as a less than scary children's character, selling cereal as "Count Chocula" and teaching preschoolers their numbers

Mummy Dearest

Strictly speaking, **mummies** are not mythological creatures. Or at least, they never used to be. A mummy is a whole corpse—flesh, bones, and skin—that has been preserved in some fashion. The usual methods are by chemicals, extreme dryness (desiccation), freezing, or lack of exposure to air. Well-preserved bodies many centuries old have been discovered in the airless peat bogs of Great Britain. And frozen, 1600-year-old mummies of aboriginal Alaskans still bear intact, soot-filled tattoos etched into their skin.

Say the word *mummy*, however, and the modern image is that of a human form wrapped in strips of white cloth, with dark holes for eyes and mouth and an uncanny ability to come alive and kill people. The image, of course, comes from the mummies most familiar to contemporary culture, those of ancient Egypt.

The Egyptians had been mummifying people since at least 4000 BCE. This involved removing the internal organs, then stuffing body cavities with ointments, a salt called **natron,** and balsamic herbs before winding the remains with linen strips. The practice continued until around 700 BCE.

Eventually Europeans discovered that Egyptian mummies contained resins that resembled a type of rare crude oil then in strong demand as a medicine. (The oil was called **mummeia,** from which the word *mummy* is derived.)

Enterprising businessmen were looting Egyptian tombs and exporting mummies to be ground up and consumed as a mummeia substitute by the 1400s. But the discovery of boy king Tutankhamen's tomb in 1922 brought worldwide attention to mummies. Public interest further skyrocketed after a series of strange deaths occurred among those connected with opening the tomb. King Tut's mummy appeared cursed.

Only 10 years after Tut's tomb discovery, the first Hollywood film portraying the mummy as a cursed monster hit American movie theaters. Universal Pictures' *The Mummy*, released in 1932, was followed by *The Mummy's Hand* in 1940, *The Mummy's Tomb,* 1942, *The Mummy's Ghost,* 1944, and *The Mummy's Curse,* 1945.

Comedians have also exploited the potential for humor in the wrapped-up, staggering corpses; one of the earliest films to poke fun was the comedy *Abbot and Costello Meet the Mummy* in 1955. And mummy film collectors avidly seek out foreign and independent movies such as an offering from Mexico titled *Robot Versus the Aztec Mummy*. In more recent years, mummy movies have become blockbuster hits with Universal's 1999 remake of *The Mummy*, its 2001 sequel, *The Mummy Returns*, and 2008's *The Mummy: Tomb of the Dragon Emperor*, all starring Brendan Fraser.

The amazing fact is that in less than 100 years, mummies have gone from ancient funerary relics to vengeful, undead monsters wreaking havoc and unleashing dark curses. But this may not be the end of the mummy's evolution. Strange as it may seem, a company in Salt Lake City has pioneered a modern method of mummification that preserves corpses as soft tissue in hopes that one day, they may be cloned and reborn with former memories intact.

Summum Corporation operates from a golden, pyramid-shaped building, and has over 27,000 people waiting to be mummified by their patented process. The service costs between $60,000 and $350,000, and the company's founder, Corky Ra, says many celebrities have already ponied up the exorbitant fees in hopes of achieving immortality.[10] The company has preserved hundreds of cats and dogs. And if future scientists really can bring back the remains of today's movie stars and millionaires, mummies may just have the last, mournful, hollow laugh after all.

as "The Count" on the TV show, *Sesame Street*. Vampire Halloween costumes for toddlers, cats, and dogs are common. These images, of course, are based on Bram Stoker's count, which may have been partially based on the fifteenth century Romanian prince named Vlad Tepes, or "Vlad the Impaler."

Although he became famous for killing hundreds of people by impaling them on poles and for committing many other gruesome atrocities, Vlad was not known for drinking blood. He did, however, appropriately inherit the title of "Dracul," or Dracula, which means "devil," from his ruthless father. Stoker discovered the name while researching his novel, and one of the cruelest monarchs ever to rule in Europe became forever linked with the mythic, caped figure that is now a pop icon.

Reinventing the Revenant

New generations continually spawn updated versions of the undead. Joss Whedon's TV shows *Buffy the Vampire Slayer* (1997-2003) and *Angel* (1999-2004) featured a romantic, "good guy" vamp as well as legions of fiendish night stalkers. Novelist Anne Rice's best-selling *Interview with the Vampire*, *The Vampire Lestat*, and other books in her series *The Vampire Chronicles* captured the public's imagination, and added to the modern view of vampires as sympathetic characters—especially after popular actors Tom Cruise and Brad Pitt starred in the movie based on her book.

Author Stephanie Meyer's recent teen series that started with her book, *Twilight*, casts vampires as the ultimate in romantic boyfriends. A movie adaptation became a big hit in 2008.

It's little wonder, then, that a modern subculture of self-proclaimed **vampyres** exists in the Western world today, with social networks in most major cities and online. Some participants in this widely varying movement may actually drink the blood of cooperative acquaintances, and many dress in capes, black clothing, and white makeup. Perhaps they themselves will one day become the stuff of legends, as memories of their activities grow and morph through time. After all, as we have seen in cases from ancient reptiles-turned-dragons to Viking berserkers-become-werewolves, time tends to smudge the supposedly sharp line between myth and reality.

Timeline

c. 6000 BCE   In Catal Hüyük, an ancient city of present southern Turkey, artists depict sacred bulls and priests wearing animal skins in wall murals.

c. 4000   Egyptians are known to practice sophisticated mummification of their dead.

c. 3500   A Babylonian artwork shows a unicorn fighting a lion.

c. 3100   The Egyptians depict fantastic creatures like the serpopard and griffin in their art.

c. 2697   First Chinese emperor with a face said to resemble a dragon's face.

c. 2500   Unicorns appear on clay seals in Moenjo-Daro (present-day Pakistan).

c. 2000   Mesopotamian *Epic of Gilgamesh* includes Enkidu, a hairy character that is half man, half bull.

c. 1750   The Kassites of ancient Iran carve the first known centaurs onto stone boundary markers.

c. 1400   The Great Sphinx of Giza is constructed in Egypt (traditional date).

c. 1000   Estimated time that the giant, stylized horse or dragon was cut into the chalk rise at Dragon Hill near Uffington, England, where the dragon slain by St. George was rumored to be buried.

c. 1000   The Adena, an Amerindian people whose skeletons show they were significantly taller than other indigenous people of the time, begin to flourish.

c. 1000–800   The Assyrians depict demigod bird-man, Pazuzu.

c. 800   Greek writer Aristeas makes the first written reference to griffins.

c. 700   The Greek poet Homer immortalizes many ancient legends of Greek mythology in his poems *The Odyssey* and *The Iliad*.

c. 650   Paintings of the Chimera, part human, goat, and lion, appear in Greek art.

c. 450   Greek doctor Ctésias describes a race of dog-headed people in India.

c. 400   Greek physician Mnemon writes about the manticore.

c. 400   A Thracian helmet shows a "rider god" on horseback.

c. 100   Greek writer Plutarch tells of the grylli, men with the heads of pigs and a human face set into their stomachs.

c. 55   Romans destroy the Syrian temple of mermaid goddess Atargatis.

c. 20   The Roman poet Virgil writes *The Aenid*, with giant sea snakes that attack a man and his sons in Troy.

c. 50 CE   Roman Pliny the Elder describes how to make a unicorn by twisting young ox horns together, and writes of mermaids as if they are real creatures.

c. 300   Approximate time of the Christian martyr St. Christopher, often depicted as a dog-headed man.

c. 300   St. George the dragon slayer saves the Libyan town of Silene from a dragon, according to legend.

c. 558   Fisherman catches a mermaid near Lough Neagh in Scotland.

c. 900   Europeans begin mistaking narwhal horns for unicorn horns and grind them into medicine.

1100–1200   The scitalis, a serpent-like dragon, appeared in bestiaries of Europe.

1218   The older serpent and rooster forms of the basilisk merge into a combination creature in a popular bestiary, or description of beasts.

c. 1300   Descriptions appear of a Chinese unicorn called a ki-lin.

c. 1300 Explorer Marco Polo describes the roc, a giant bird, as a native animal of Madagascar, and says a race of dog-headed people live off the coast of India.

1500 Italian poet Ludvico Ariosto writes the poem *Orlando Furioso*, which popularizes the hippogriff.

1500 European sailors begin describing sea hogs, creatures with the tail of a fish but the front legs, head, and tusks of a hog.

1500 European writers report that the bones of a giant, Druon Antigoon, who stood 18 feet tall, lie in the castle at Antwerp, Belgium; the bones are later proved to be those of a whale.

1578 The nine-foot-three man, John Middleton, known as "The Childe of Hale," was born in England.

1700s Kaffir tribesmen produce faux unicorns from cattle.

1730s, late Vampire hunts, which lead to prosecution of citizens for grave desecration, are carried out on the Croatian island of Lastovo.

1735 Date "cursed" child was said to have been born in New Jersey, believed to be the origin of the Jersey Devil legend.

1789 A pair of tatzelwurms give a man in the Swiss Alps a heart attack and began a legend that continues into present times.

1800s, early Nancy Young, a teenager who died of a contagious respiratory disease, is exhumed after burial and becomes known as the Vampire of Foster, Rhode Island.

1800–1850 Washington eagle, now extinct, is sighted across the United States by observers, including John James Audubon.

1819 John Polidori writes pioneer vampire novel, *The Vampyre*.

1847 Novel *Varney the Vampire*, written as 220 short serial stories, is published.

1869 In Cardiff, New York, the carved stone hoax called the Cardiff giant is "discovered" in a farmer's field and presented to the world as a petrified giant.

1886 The *Tombstone Epitaph* publishes a story, but no photo, about two ranchers who shot a pterodactyl-like bird.

1897   Landmark vampire novel, Bram Stoker's *Dracula*, is published.

1900s, early   The Black Dog of Ardura appears on the Island of Mull in the Hebrides.

1909   Dozens of witnesses in Pennsylvania and New Jersey report seeing a ram-headed, screaming, hoofed, flying creature dubbed the Jersey Devil.

1912   Westerners first learn of the Komodo dragon in Indonesia.

1918   American giant Robert Wadlow, who stood eight-foot-eleven-and-one-half, is born in Alton, Illinois.

1920s   The kongamato, a large, leathery-winged, flying creature, is reported in Zambia and Rhodesia.

1922   King Tutankhamen's tomb is opened in Egypt, and resulting disasters suggest the mummy's "curse."

1928   Fantasy/horror writer H.P. Lovecraft publishes "The Call of Cthulhu" about a giant, squid-like alien that came to earth in prehistoric times; Cthulhu has now reached mythic status among some Lovecraft fans.

1932   Hollywood film *The Mummy* helps turn ancient Egyptian mummies from funeral relics to horrific monsters.

1933   Dr. W. Franklin Dove at the University of Maine produces a calf unicorn by means of a tissue graft.

1938   The movie *The Wizard of Oz* puts vivid images of flying monkeys, a type of chimera, into the public imagination.

1939   Norwegian folk tale is told of a contemporary farmer who used a magic wolf skin to turn into a wolf.

1961   Mermaid sighting is reported in the Irish Sea's Isle of Man.

1966–1967   Mothman terrorizes inhabitants of Mount Pleasant, West Virginia.

1970s   The role-playing fantasy game *Dungeons and Dragons* popularizes dragons, trolls, demons, and other mythical monsters of the past.

1976 Texas man Armando Grimaldo claimed to have almost been carried off by a man-sized, leathery-winged creature.

1980 A couple named Ravenheart-Zell release a photo of a white unicorn goat created using tissue grafts.

1980s–1990s The animated children's cartoon *My Pretty Pony* features two unicorns.

1991 The newspaper article "The Beast of Bray Road" breaks news of a local "werewolf" in *The Week*, a Walworth County, Wisconsin, newspaper based in Delavan.

1993 Aswang Productions releases a film, *The Aswang*, about a Philippine vampire of folk legend.

1995 The Puerto Rican chupacabras, or goat-sucker, comes to worldwide attention after many sightings and reports of animals drained of blood.

1997 University of Massachusetts research team successfully grafts cow cartilage resembling a human ear onto the back of a mouse.

2002–2004 California man, "John," reports three visitations by a phantom black hound, each at a time when his life was in jeopardy.

2003 Chinese team combines human cells with rabbit eggs to create a human/animal chimera.

2004 Man and wife claim to see Washington eagle on the Mississippi River near Stillwater, Minnesota.

2004 Minnesota's Mayo Clinic produces pigs with human blood; Ocean University of China combines two tropical fish species into one chimera.

2005 New Yorker Stuart Newman's request for a human/ape hybrid patent is rejected.

2006 Two Wisconsin men see a humanoid with bat wings dive at their truck near LaCrosse, Wisconsin.

2006 A two-headed turtle is found in an animal market of the Chinese city of Qingdao.

2007   University of Nevada professor produces a sheep with enough human organs growing inside of it to be pronounced 15 percent human.

2007   A pet bearded dragon named Zak-n-Wheezie is born in California with two heads.

2008   A pet bearded dragon with two heads is born in Kernersville, North Carolina.

2008   Catholic bishops in the British Isles demand right-to-life for human/animal chimera embryos.

Endnotes

INTRODUCTION

1. Janet Cave, ed., *Mysteries of the Unknown: Mysterious Creatures* (Alexandria, Va: Time-Life books, 1988), 7.

2. Veronica Ions, *Indian Mythology* (London, England: Drury House, 1967).

CHAPTER 1

1. David Adams Leeming, "The Chimera," In *Mythical and Fabulous Creatures: A Sourcebook and Research Guide* (New York: Peter Bedrick Books, 1988), 59.

2. Ibid.,108.

3. Maryann Mott, "Animal-Human Hybrids Spark Controversy," National Geographic News, http://news.nationalgeographic.com/news/pf/62295276.html (Posted January 25, 2005).

4. Claudia Joseph, "Now Scientists Create a Sheep that's 15% Human," *Daily Mail*, http://www.dailymail.co.uk/pages/text/print.html?in_article_id=444436&in_page_id=1770 (Posted March 24, 2007).

5. Karen Macklin, "Clone Home: Jellyfish DNA in a Rabbit? It's science; it's art; it's 'Gene(sis)' at the Berkeley Art Museum," *SF Weekly*, http://www.ekac.org/sfweekly2003.html (Posted September 3, 2003).

6. Casey Sorrow, "Patent attempted for human and ape lab chimeras," Monkeys in the News, http://monkeydaynews.blogspot.com/2005/02/patent-attempted-for-human-and-ape-lab.html (Posted February 14, 2005).

7. Jonathan Petre, "Chimera embryos have right to life, say bishops," *Telegraph News*, http://www.telegraph.co.uk/news/uknews/1555639/Chimera-embryos-have-right-to-life%2C-say-bishops.html (Posted June 19, 2008).

8. Donald B. Redford, ed., *The Oxford Essential Guide to Egyptian Mythology* (New York: Berkley Books, 2003), 117.

CHAPTER 2

1. Theony Condos, *Star Myths of the Greeks and Romans: A Source Book* (Grand Rapids, Mich.: Phanes Press, 1997), 154.

2. David Bellingham, *An Introduction to Celtic Mythology* (Edison, N.J.: Chartwell Books, 2002), 59.

3. Unicorns.com, http://www.unicorns.com (Downloaded November 12, 2008).

4. Norma Gaffron, *Unicorns: Great Mysteries, Opposing Viewpoints* (San Diego, Calif.: Greenhaven Press, 1989), 71.

5. Ibid., 44.

6. Peter Costello, *The Magic Zoo, the Natural History of Fabulous Animals* (New York: St. Martin's Press, 1979), 97.

7. Costello, 99.

8. Jan Bonderson, *The Two-headed Boy and Other Medical Marvels* (Ithaca, N.Y.: Cornell University Press, 2004), 137.

9. C.J.S. Thompson, *The Mystery and Lore of Monsters* (New Hyde Park, N.Y.: University Books, 1968), 62.

10. Ibid.

11. D.J. Conway, *Magickal Mystical Creatures* (Woodbury, Minn.: Llewellyn Publications, 2005), 48.

12. Reimund Kvideland and Henning K. Sehmsdorf, eds., *Scandinavian Folk Belief and Legend* (Minneapolis, Minn.: University of Minnesota, 1988), 90.

13. Costello, 164–165.

CHAPTER 3

1. Linda S. Godfrey, *Strange Wisconsin: More Badger State Weirdness* (Madison, Wis.: Trails Books, 2007), 52–54.

2. D.J. Conway, *Magical Mystical Creatures* (Woodbury, Minn.: Lewellyn Publications, 2005), 87.

3. Ibid.

4. Malcolm South, ed., *Mythical and Fabulous Creatures: A Sourcebook and Resource Guide* (New York: Peter Bedrick Books, 1988), 148.

5. Paul Murgatroyd, *Mythical Monsters in Classical Literature* (London, England: Gerald Duckworth & Co., 2007), 44.

6. Sam D. Gill and Irene F. Sullivan, *Dictionary of Native American Mythology* (New York: Oxford University Press, 1992), 303.

7. Troy Taylor, *Weird Illinois: Your Travel Guide to Illinois' Local Legends and Best Kept Secrets* (New York: Sterling Publishing, 2005), 88–89.

8. South, 59.

9. Ibid., 85.

10. Costello, 74.

11. Ibid., 79.

12. Mark Sceurman and Mark Moran, *Weird New Jersey: Your Travel Guide to New Jersey's Local Legends and Best Kept Secrets,* (New York: Barnes & Noble, 2003), 104–105.

13. Land of the Devil, "Something Follows Campers in Sussex County," Land of the Devil Web site, http://www.landofthedevil.com/Subtopics/Sightings/sighting3.html (Posted August 20, 2007).

14. Hoag Levins, "Halloween Crossed with History," Historic Camden County, http://historiccamdencounty.com/ccnews18.shtml (Posted on October 29, 2001).

15. Loren Coleman, *Mothman and Other Curious Encounters* (New York: Paraview Press, 2002), 38.

16. Scott Maruna, "Substantiating Audubon's Washington Eagle," Biofort Blog, http://biofort.blogspot.com/2006/10/substantiating-audubons-washington.html (Posted October 14, 2006).

17. Scott Maruna, "Witness Claims a Washington Eagle Sighting," Biofort Blog, http://biofort. blogspot.com/2006/10/witness-claims-washington-eagle.html (Posted October 23, 2006).

18. Colin Bord and Janet Bord, *Creatures from Elsewhere* (London, England: Orbis Publishing, 1984), 24.

19. Bernard Heuvelmans, "Lingering Pterodactyls, Part One," trans. Chorvinsky, *Strange Magazine* 6 (1990): 8.

20. Karl P. N. Shuker, "The Search for the Thunderbird Photo," *Strange Magazine* 20 (December 1998): 44–45.

21. Ibid.

CHAPTER 4

1. "Beltsville Agricultural Research Center," United States Department of Agriculture Agricultural Research Service, http://www.ars. usda.gov/is/AR/archive/oct01/ba rc1001.htm (Accessed February 19, 2008).

2. Janie McHugh, "Legend of the Goatman still lives on in Bowie and around the world," The Bowie Blade-News, http://www. hometownbowie.com/news/ blade/2007/10/18-35 (Posted October 18, 2007).

3. Matt Lake, *Weird Maryland, Your Travel Guide to Maryland's Local Legends and Best Kept Secrets* (New York: Sterling Publishing, 2006), 77–79.

4. Patricia Dale-Green, *Lore of the Dog* (Boston: Houghton Mifflin Co., 1967), 5.

5. Dora-Jane Hamblin, *The First Cities* (New York: Time-Life Books, 1973), 43.

6. Malcolm South, ed., *Mythical and Fabulous Creatures* (New York: Peter Bedrick Books, 1987), 354.

7. Ibid.

8. Ibid., 225–226.

9. Ibid., 134.

10. Costello, 35.

11. Ibid., 37.

12. Ibid., 38.

13. "Devil," *Funk & Wagnall's New Encyclopedia*, Vol. 7 (New York: Funk & Wagnall's Inc., 1979), 452.

14. Ibid., 453.

15. Ronan Coghlan, *A Dictionary of Cryptozoology* (Bangor, Northern Ireland: Xiphos Books, 2004), 160.

16. Richard Ellis, *Monsters of the Sea* (New York: Alfred A. Knopf, 1994), 109.

CHAPTER 5

1. Marc Alexander, *The Sutton Companion to British Folklore, Myths and Legends* (Gloucestershire, United Kingdom: Sutton Publishing, 2005), 300.

2. Carol Rose, *Giants, Monsters and Dragons* (New York: W.W. Norton and Co., 2001), 360.

3. Charles Gould, *Mythical Monsters* (Detroit, Mich.: Singing Tree Press, reissue 1969), 219.

4. Ibid., 399.

5. "Tatzelwurm," Unknown Explorers Online Resources, http://www.unknownexplorers. com/tatzelwurm.php (Accessed September 4, 2008).

6. Rose, 346.

7. Costello, 126.

8. Pliny the Elder, *The Natural History*, trans. John Bostock and H.T. Riley, Esq. (London, England: Taylor and Francis, 1855), chap. 20. Also available online at http://www.perseus.tufts.edu/hopper/text.jsp?doc=Perseus:text:1999.02.0137:book=29:chapter=20&highlight=remedies%2Cdragon (Downloaded September 9, 2008).

9. South, 38.

10. Ibid., 122.

CHAPTER 6

1. Rose, 250.

2. Sam D. Gill and Irene F. Sullivan, *Dictionary of Native American Mythology* (New York: Oxford University Press, 1992), 192.

3. Rose, 250.

4. Betty Sodders, *Michigan Prehistory Mysteries* (Au Train, Mich.: Avery Color Studios, 1990), 66.

5. H.A. Guerber, *The Book of the Epic*, http://www.ebooksread.com/authors-eng/h-a-guerber/the-book-of-the-epic-8-3/page-19-the-book-of-the-epic-8-3.shtml (Downloaded September 11, 2008).

6. Rose, 235.

7. John Bailey and Rose Quigley, *Nellie Longarms Will Get You if You Don't Watch Out* (Nantwich, U.K.: Quayside Creative, 2007).

8. H.P. Lovecraft, "The Call of Cthulhu." *Tales of the Cthulhu Mythos*, Vol. 1, ed. August Derleth (New York: Ballantine Books, 1969), 29.

9. Joyce Carol Oates, ed., *Tales of H.P. Lovecraft* (New York: The Ecco Press, 2000), XIV.

CHAPTER 7

1. J.K. Rowling, *Harry Potter and the Sorcerer's Stone* (New York: Scholastic Press, 1998).

2. Diana Marcum, "Leapin' Lizards! Valley couple's two-headed oddity of nature truly is one in a million – believe it or not," The Fresno Bee, http://www.fresnobee.com/907/story/699961.html (Posted June 29, 2008).

3. Sean Markey, "Photo in the News: Two-Headed Turtle Found in China," National Geographic News, http://news.nationalgeographic.com/news/2006/03/0317_060317_two_headed.html (Posted September 3, 2008).

4. World Culture Encyclopedia, "Mountain Arapesh: Religion and Expressive Culture," Every Culture, http://www.everyculture.com/Oceania/Mountain-Arapesh-Religion-and-Expressive-Culture.html (Downloaded September 27, 2008).

5. Ronan Coghlan, *A Dictionary of Cryptozoology* (Bangor, Northern Ireland: Xiphos Books, 2004), 239.

6. Rose, 9.

CHAPTER 8

1. Gill, 345.

2. Jim Miles, "Pygmies and Giants," *FATE Magazine* (March 1985): 38.

3. Ruben De Somer, "Real Giants in the Low Countries?" *FATE Magazine* (January 2004): 22–27.

4. *The NIV Study Bible*, Genesis 6:4, (Grand Rapids, Mich.: Zondervan, 1985), 14.

5. Rose, 286.

6. Rachel Cotterell and Arthur Storm, *The Ultimate Encyclopedia of Mythology* (London: Anness Publishing, 2006), 306–307.

7. *The NIV Study Bible*, 401.

8. South, 302.

9. C.J.S. Thompson, *The Mystery and Lore of Monsters* (New Hyde Park, N.Y.: University Books, 1968), 143.

10. David M. Jones and Brian L. Molyneaux, *Mythology of the American Nations* (London, England: Anness Publishing, 2006), 110.

11. South, 204.

12. Alex Boese, "Cardiff Giant," Museum of Hoaxes, http://www.museumofho axes.com/hoax/Hoaxipedia/Cardiff_Giant/ (Downloaded October 2, 2008).

CHAPTER 9

1. Donald B. Redford, ed., *The Oxford Essential Guide to Egyptian Mythology* (New York: Berkley Books, 2003), 21.

2. Patricia Dale-Green, *Lore of the Dog* (Boston: Houghton Mifflin, 1967), 50–51.

3. Ibid., 55.

4. Reimund Kvideland and Henning K. Sehmsdorf, eds., *Scandinavian Folk Belief and Legend* (Minneapolis, Minn.: University of Minnesota Press, 1988), 78.

5. Linda S. Godfrey, *The Beast of Bray Road: Tailing Wisconsin's Werewolf* (Madison, Wis.: Trails Books, 2003).

6. Linda S. Godfrey, *Hunting the American Werewolf* (Madison, Wis.: Trails Books, 2006).

7. Rosemary Ellen Guiley, *The Encyclopedia of Vampires, Werewolves, and Other Monsters* (New York: Checkmark Books, 2005), 334.

8. Ibid., 176.

9. Neil Arnold, *Monster: The A-Z of Zooform Phenomena* (North Devon, U.K.: CFZ Publishing, 2007), 151-156.

10. Ron Laytner, "The Mummy Makers," Edit International, http://www.editinternationa l.com/read.php?id=47ddcf51d5a3e (Downloaded October 17, 2008).

Glossary

AI TOJON A double-headed eagle in the lore of the Yakut people of Siberia that was known for creating light

AILLEN TRECHENN A three-headed Irish monster that inhabited an ancient burial mound and attacked humans on Celtic holidays

ALICORN A name for unicorn horn, especially in Europe's Middle Ages, when ground into a medicinal powder, and now believed to have been produced from the spiral horn of a narwhal

ANUBIS An Egyptian god of the underworld with a human body and the head of a jackal, considered the patron god of embalmers

ASWANG A Philippine vampire that looks either like a flying head or old woman that vampirizes unborn children with a very long tongue

ATARGATIS A mermaid goddess worshipped by ancient Syrians and Philistines at least up to the end of the first century BCE

ATLAS A Greek giant, son of one of the Titans, known for his job of supporting the sky on his shoulders

BASILISK A creature part serpent and part rooster, also known in medieval Europe as a cockatrice, and said to kill or turn to stone anything it breathed upon; could be defeated by its own reflection in a mirror

BEAST OF BRAY ROAD A nickname for the upright, man-sized, wolf-headed creature first publicly reported in the vicinity of Bray Road outside of Elkhorn, Wisconsin

BELLEROPHON Greek hero who defeated the Chimera with the help of Pegasus

BERSERKERS Norse warriors who donned the skins of wolves or bears to appear fearsome in battle and to magically take on bear-like or wolf-like characteristics, and who, according to legend, could also transform into the animals whose skins they wore

BESTIARY An illustrated book of known and mythical beasts, their lore, and moral significance and status, popular in the Middle Ages

BICEPHALIC A creature with two heads

BLACK DOG OF ARDURA A phantom dog that has appeared on the island of Mull in the Inner Hebrides since the early 1900s

BLACK SHUCK (BLACK SHUG) In the British Isles, localized names for hellhounds, phantom black dogs that appear at times of death or peril

BOVINE Referring to or related to cattle

BUCENTAUR A creature of Greek and Roman mythology with a human head and torso growing out of the four-legged body of a bull

BUNYAN, PAUL Mythological giant of North American lumber camps, known for humorous stories of exaggerated feats

CACUS In Greek and Roman mythology, a huge creature with a body like a spider, three human heads branching from one long neck, and long, thick legs

CARDIFF GIANT A hoax perpetrated in New York state in 1869 involving a 10-foot stone carving of a human figure, intended to ridicule belief in giants of the Bible

CENTAUR A creature of Greek and Roman mythology with a human head and torso growing out of the four-legged body of a horse

CENTICORE Also known as the yale, a spotted horse-like animal with a goat head and elephant tail, described by Romans but still popular in medieval times and believed to be able to rotate its two horns in battle

CERBERUS In Greek and Roman mythology, a giant dog with three or more heads who stood guard at the entrance to the underworld, or Hades

CHEMOSIT A flesh-eating, man-bird creature of East African tradition, unusual in that it is portrayed with nine sets of buttocks

CHIMERA   Originally a Greek monster that combined parts of a lion, a goat, and a serpent's tail, but the word now also means any fantastic animal, especially those made up of more than one type of animal; in science, it denotes an animal containing DNA from more than one individual

CHIRON   A learned centaur, half man and half horse, in Greek mythology who was considered a benevolent teacher of many heroes and scholars

CHUPACABRAS   A flying, three-clawed, spiny-backed creature whose name means "goat-sucker" in Spanish, seen in Puerto Rico and much of the Americas and known for draining the blood of farm animals

COCKATRICE   See BASILISK

CONCHEANNAICH   An ancient dog-headed tribe of Ireland

CTHULHU   A vast, alien creature with a squid-like, tentacled head; a dragon body; and immense, bat-like wings invented as part of the "Old Ones" race by early twentieth century horror fiction writer H.P. Lovecraft, and now possessed of its own mythology and cult following

CUTANEOUS HORN   Grown from skin cells, as in the cutaneous facial horn of the French woman, Madame DiManche

CYCLOPES (CYCLOPS)   In Greek and Roman mythology, one-eyed gigantic beings who helped Zeus and were originally creative and benevolent but who degenerated to eat human flesh

CYNOCEPHALI   Dog-headed humans thought by explorer Marco Polo and Greek writer Ctésias to exist near India

DEVIL   A being of supreme evil of the Jewish, Christian, and Muslim faiths, also known as Satan, usually shown as a red-skinned man with the horns, legs, and hooves of a goat

DRACULA   A word meaning "devil" that was a nickname of the bloodthirsty fifteenth century Wallachian prince, Vlad Tepes, and also the name of the Transylvanian count in author Bram Stoker's 1897 novel of the same name

DRAGON HILL Also Uffington Hill, a mound located near Berkshire, England, that bears a 365-foot prehistoric or Celtic figure that resembles a dragon or a galloping horse

DRAKON Greek dragons, one of whose teeth provided warriors for the hero Cadmus when planted, and another that had to be defeated by the hero Jason in his quest for the golden fleece

DRUON ANTIGOON A legendary giant of Antwerp, Belgium, thought to be 18 feet tall and who maimed those who would not pay a fee to cross the nearby river

ECHIDNE OR ECHIDNA A cave-dwelling female monster in Greek mythology with a woman's upper body but whose lower half was a serpent

ECH-USHKYA A vicious form of Scottish waterhorse (shape-shifter) that devoured its victims after luring them into a pond and drowning them

ENKIDU A half man, half beast creature usually shown with the fur and horns of a bull, who fought and then befriended the hero Gilgamesh in a Mesopotamian epic of about 2000 BCE

FAUN (FAUNI, PL.) The goatman offspring of the Roman god of rural land, Faunus, known to sneak into bedrooms at night to induce nightmares

FAUNA Animals of a certain place or time

FAUNUS The Roman god of rural land and agriculture, usually shown as a goatman

FENG-HUANG A Chinese version of the firebird or phoenix, a great holy bird with flame-colored feathers, associated with the sun

GANESHA A Hindu deity with the pot-bellied body of a man and the head of an elephant

GARGOYLE A grotesque creature such as a winged chimera carved onto a waterspout, best known from medieval European cathedrals and intended to scare away evil spirits

GARUDA A Hindu god of India, shown as a great, eagle-like bird or half-bird, half-human; known as The Devourer, he was the enemy of the serpents called Nagas

GIANTS   In Greek mythology, mortal giants with snake tails who battled the gods of Olympus and Zeus but were defeated by Heracles

GIGANTISM   A medical condition caused when the pituitary gland overproduces growth hormone, resulting in stature much taller than normal human height

GILGAMESH   The hero of a Mesopotamian epic from about 2000 BCE

GOATMAN   The Goatman of Prince George's County, a half-man, half-goat creature of the rural areas of Virginia, north of Washington, D.C., that was created by government genetic experiments and roams the area, preying on livestock and pets

GOLD-MAKER   A great bird of India that could make gold by mixing its droppings with sand

GOLIATH   A giant in the Old Testament of the Bible who was a champion of the Philistine army and was defeated by the future king, David, who wielded only a stone and slingshot

GORGON   One of three monster sisters, sometimes shown with wings, whose giant teeth and serpents-for-hair turned onlookers to stone in Greek and Roman mythology

GRIFFIN (GRYPHON)   A combination of an eagle's head and wings with the body of a lion, known in Greek legend as a guardian of gold treasure and often used in European coats of arms

GRYLLUS   A Greek and Roman monster with the head of a pig, a man-like body, and a second, human face set into its stomach that according to Greek legend was created by a sorceress named Circe

GYRTRASH   Another name for hellhound in the British Isles

HANUMAN   In Hindu mythology of India, a giant, inquisitive monkey who demonstrates extreme loyalty to the god Rama but also may represent greed

HARPIES   Monsters with the head and upper torso of a woman but wings and legs of a large bird, known for snatching away enemies of the Greek gods

HELLHOUND   A phantom dog, usually black, that often appears at times of death or sickness, especially in church yards and crossroads

HIPPOCAMP   A creature of Greek mythology with the foreparts of a horse and rear quarters like a sea serpent's tail, used to pull Poseidon's chariot

HIPPOGRIFF   A variation of the griffin, with an eagle's wings and head, a lion's forequarters and a horse's rear quarters, derived mainly from European tales and poems of the Middle Ages

HYDRA   A dragon-like creature of Greek and Roman mythology with up to 1,000 heads, one of which was immortal; the rest had the power to grow two replacements if severed

HYDRIPPUS   A creature of Greek mythology that was half horse, half fish

JERSEY DEVIL   A legendary creature of the New Jersey Pine Barrens with sightings claimed from 1735 to present, said to resemble a kangaroo with fangs, leathery wings, and hooves on its hind feet

JORMUNGAND   In Norse mythology, a serpent-monster, sired by the gods Loki and Angrboda, that grew large enough to encircle the earth and would eventually play a part in Ragnarok, the final battle that ends the world

KARKADANN   A unicorn of Arabian legend that resembled an antelope and bore a single, curved horn

KI-LIN   A unicorn-like Chinese creature that resembled a bull with a single curved horn, dating from at least the Ming Dynasty circa the late 1300s-1600s CE

KOMODO DRAGON   A carnivorous monitor lizard that is native to Indonesia and may reach lengths of 12 feet or more

KONGAMATO   A large, leathery-winged flying creature of Zambia and Rhodesia that resembled a pteranodon; reported in the 1920s, it was described as red-skinned, with a wingspan of four to seven feet

LAMBTON WORM   A serpent-like dragon that terrorized the Northumbria region of England around 1100 CE

LAMIA   In Greek mythology, the goddess consort of Zeus who became a demonic type of vampire especially known for sucking the blood of infants after Hera, wife of Zeus, killed Lamia's children

LILITH   In Hebrew mythology, the first wife of Adam who became a winged demon and preyed like a vampire on newborn babies

LUNG   A class of Chinese dragons with scales, four legs, and very long tails, who guarded the waters of the earth

LYCANTHROPES (LYCANS)   People who believe that they transform into wolves and take on many of the wolf's characteristics

MAN BAT   A man-sized, furry creature with a bat-like wingspread of 10 feet, sighted by witnesses near LaCrosse, Wisconsin, in 2006

MANIMAL   A creature that is part man, part animal

MANTA   A flat-bodied, tentacled, many-eyed sea creature of Chilean folklore

MANTICORE   A sphinx-like fantasy creature of medieval times with a lion's body, human head, wings, and a tail that shot barbed stingers

MARES OF DIOMEDES   In Greek mythology, four giant, man-eating mares who belonged to the giant Diomedes and were tamed when the hero Heracles fed them the giant's flesh

MEDUSA   One of the Greek Gorgons, who were three sisters with snakes for hair, giant fangs, and a gaze that turned people to stone

MERMAID AND MERMEN   Creatures with human heads and torsos but having fish tails instead of legs, in legends dating back to the earliest civilizations

MINOTAUR   A Greek creature half man and half bull that lived in the middle of a giant maze called the Labyrinth on the island of Crete until slain by the hero Theseus

MISHIPESHU   The water lynx, a horned, long-tailed, cat-like creature believed by the Ojibwe and Menominee (Ho Chunk) people to guard underground springs and to war with the thunderbirds

MISIGANEBIC   A green, serpent-like creature believed by some Native American tribes to live at the bottom of North American lakes, and whose job it is to keep the lakes clean

MISIKINIPIK   A serpent-like being of immeasurable size, believed by Cree nations to prowl beneath earth and sea

MONKFISH   A fish whose cape-like torso and bald crown, claimed sailors of the Middle Ages, resembled those of a Roman Catholic monk

MOSHIRIIKKWECHEP   The Japanese giant trout who could hold the world on its back and must be perpetually restrained in sea mud to prevent its causing earthquakes

MOTHMAN   A human-sized, winged creature with large red eyes and no visible neck seen by hundreds of people around Point Pleasant, Virginia, in the 1960s

MUMMEIA   A type of crude oil that bubbled to the surface in parts of Europe and was widely prized as a medicine in the Middle Ages and beyond

MUMMY (MUMMIES)   A corpse preserved in its entirety by means of chemicals, freezing, or lack of exposure to moisture or air

MUSPEL (SURT)   Norse fire giant destined to burn all living creatures at the end of the world

NATRON   A type of salt used in Egyptian mummification of human and animal bodies

NELLIE LONGARMS   In contemporary British folklore, an inland water hag with green teeth and seaweed-like hair, used as a bogey-figure to warn children away from dangerous ponds

NEPHILIM   In Hebrew, "the fallen ones," thought to be people of large stature who lived before the great flood

OANNES   A Babylonian god who came from the sea to bring the knowledge of architecture, agriculture, writing, and other gifts of civilization, described as part man and part fish

OG (PALET)   A giant of Hebrew legend said to have survived the great flood either because of his height or by riding atop Noah's ark; also connected with the King of Bashan in the Old Testament

OGRE   A malicious giant, often the villain of fairy tales, and usually malformed, brutish, and an eater of human flesh

ONI   A Chinese demon from the Buddhist tradition, with either the head of a horse or an ox, horned, and giant in size, possibly having three eyes

PALET See OG.

PAN The Greek god of nature who resembled satyrs or goatmen, and was famed for his musical talent for playing flutes

P'AN KU A giant Chinese man-god whose body became that country's five sacred mountains

PAZUZU A winged demon-god of ancient Assyria, with a canine face and as many as four wings

PEGASUS In Greek mythology, a great winged horse whose father was the sea god Poseidon and whose mother was the Gorgon monster, Medusa

PHOENIX A giant bird symbolizing rebirth due to its ability to self-immolate at the end of its life, then rise anew from its own ashes

PIASA A giant bird monster painted by the Illiniwek people on a cliff near Alton, Illinois, as a winged, claw-footed creature with antlers, huge fangs, and a long, skinny tail, and believed to eat human flesh

POLYCEPHALIC A creature with more than one head

POLYPHEMUS One of the better known Cyclopes of Greek mythology who lost his one eye to Odysseus as the hero rescued his men from Polyphemus' cave

POOKA (PHOUKA) The Irish version of the Scottish waterhorse, or aquatic shape-shifter, whose appearance was a bad omen

PTERANODON A genus of toothless flying reptiles of the late Cretaceous period, that fished by skimming the ocean waves and with a wingspan of 23-30 feet. The first pteranodon fossils, distinguished by their bony head crests, were found in Kansas

PTEROSAUR A term that includes all short-tailed, flying reptiles such as the genus *pteranodon*

RATU MAI BULU A huge serpent god from the Fiji Island area who could raise the sea floor to create new islands

RIGI A Micronesian giant whose upper body became the Milky Way and from whose legs all the worms of the ground were made

ROC   A great bird that figures in the Arabian tales of Sinbad the Sailor and is best known for its strength, which enabled it to carry off elephants

ST. CHRISTOPHER   A martyr of the Christian church from around 300 BCE, often shown with the head of a dog in religious art

SATYRS   Greek goat-man spirits of the forest, known for drinking and revelry

SAURIAN   An animal that resembles reptiles such as lizards, crocodiles, or dinosaurs

SCITALIS   A two-legged, winged dragon described in medieval European bestiaries, whose beautiful skin mesmerized its victims

SCYLLA   In Greek and Roman mythology, a female sea monster, once a beautiful water nymph, who lived in a cave in the Straits of Messina and who devoured sailors from passing ships

SEA DOG (SEA WOLF)   Aquatic creature of off-shore British Columbia with a canine-like head, long neck, and sometimes wings, thought by some to be mistaken sightings of leopard seals

SEA HOG   A mythical creature of about 1500 CE said by European sailors to possess the front quarters of a tusked hog and the hindquarters of a fish, later applied to porpoises taken at sea for meat

SEA SNAKES   In the Roman poet Virgil's epic poem *The Aenid*, two huge, serpentine creatures who rose up out of the sea to swallow the lone critic of the Trojan horse

SERPOPARD   An Egyptian mythical creature with a falcon head, a snake-like neck, the body of a leopard, and wings

SESHA (ANANTA SESHA, SHESHA)   The great, multiheaded world serpent of the Hindu faith, supposed to lie coiled on the ocean bottom until its heads release their venom at the end of the world

SIREN   A Greek woman-bird, sometimes bearded, feared for the ability to lure men to their deaths with their sweet song; the name later also referred to mermaids with the same skill

SLEIPNIR   In Norse mythology, an eight-legged horse ridden by the god, Odin

SPHINX   A creature combining the head of a woman, body of a lion, and wings of a bird, whose name is from a word meaning "strangler"; its form is depicted in the Great Sphinx of Giza, Egypt

STOLLENWURM   See TATZELWURM

STYMPHALIAN BIRD   Greek birds that could shoot feathers like arrows, defeated by the hero Hercules

SUMMUM CORPORATION   A company based in Salt Lake City, Utah, that has patented a modern process of human mummification

SURT   See MUSPEL

TALOS   A bronze giant who guarded the island of Crete and killed people by superheating himself, then hugging them

TATZELWURM   A creature of the Swiss Alps also known as the stollenwurm, sighted from the late 1700s to present, and having a long-tailed, lizard-like body but a cat-like face

THRACIAN   Belonging to the ancient kingdom of Thrace that included parts of present day Greece, Turkey, and Bulgaria

THUNDERBIRD   A gigantic bird, either real or in the spirit realm, held sacred by many North American indigenous peoples and believed to be able to make thunder and lightning and cause storms

TI LUNG   One of the Chinese lung, or dragons, who was given the special task of overseeing springs and flowing waters

TIAMAT   The cosmic dragon of Sumeria and Babylonia, formed from seawater, who with the god Apsu became the mother of many monstrous creatures and eventually the earth, sky, and riverways

TITANS   Greek giants whose father was Uranus and mother was Gaia, and who later helped Uranus struggle against Zeus

TLALTECUHTLI   A giant goddess of the Aztecs who was torn in half to become the earth and sky

TRITONS   A Greek race of mermaids and mermen named after Triton, son of the sea king, Poseidon

TURSUS   A Finnish folk monster with a walrus head, human torso, muscular hindquarters, and a fish-like tail, credited with helping grow the first oak tree

TWO FACES A creature of Sioux lore said to be a hairy giant with two faces and massive ears that could digest humans

TYPHON A 100-headed dragon of Greek and Roman mythology, so large that he was able to cause volcanoes after one of the gods threw a mountain on top of him, and the father of monsters such as Cerberus and the Chimera

ULLIKUMMI A Hittite giant made of diorite stone

UPELLURI Hittite giant who lived in the sea and was used as a support stand by another god to hold his growing offspring

VAMPIRE A creature that lives by draining blood or life force from other beings, often a spirit of the dead that leaves its grave to subsist off the living

VAMPIRE OF FOSTER A legend created in the 1800s in Foster, Rhode Island, when a 19-year-old dead girl, Nancy Young, was thought to have become a vampire and was exhumed

VAMPYRE The preferred spelling of people who consider themselves part of the contemporary vampire subculture

THE VAMPYRE A short novel by British doctor John Polidori that was published in 1819 and set forth many of the contemporary notions about vampires

WALINAB A term for spirit beings among the Arapesh of New Guinea

WASHINGTON EAGLE A large species of eagle reported by naturalist John James Audubon in the mid-1800s, described as having a 10-foot wingspan and russet-brown color, and thought to be presently extinct

WATERHORSE An aquatic shape-shifter of Scotland and Ireland, often appearing as a saddled horse in order to lure the unwary into rivers or ponds so it could drown them

WEREWOLF Traditionally, a human that transforms into a wolf, either physically or spiritually, usually by shamanic practices or magical means such as incantations or a belt of wolf fur

WINDIGO (WITIKO) A legendary monster of the Algonquian-speaking tribes of the northern United States and Canada, said to be tall as the trees, made partly of ice, and ravenous for human flesh

YALE   Also known as the centicore, a spotted horse-like animal with a goat head and elephant tail, described by Romans but still popular in medieval times and believed to be able to rotate its two horns in battle

YMIR   Norse frost giant whose flesh provided raw materials for the earth

ZOOMORPH   A deity with physical characteristics of an animal, or art depicting animalistic forms

Bibliography

Alexander, Marc. *The Sutton Companion to British Folklore, Myths and Legends.* Gloucestershire, United Kingdom: Sutton Publishing, 2005.

Arnold, Neil. *Monster! the A–Z of Zooform Phenomena.* North Devon, U.K.: CFZ Publishing, 2007.

Bellingham, David. *An Introduction to Celtic Mythology.* Edison, N.J.: Chartwell Books, 2002.

Boese, Alex. "Cardiff Giant," Museum of Hoaxes. Available online. URL: http://www.museumofhoaxes.com/hoax/Hoaxipedia/Cardiff_Giant/. Downloaded on October 2, 2008.

Bondeson, Jan. *The Two-headed Boy and Other Medical Marvels.* Ithaca, N.Y.: Cornell University Press, 2004.

Cave, Janet, ed. *Mysteries of the Unknown: Mysterious Creatures.* Alexandria, Va.: Time-Life Books, 1988.

Coghlan, Ronan. *A Dictionary of Cryptozoology.* Bangor, Northern Ireland: Xiphos Books, 2004.

Condos, Theony. *Star Myths of the Greeks and Romans: A Source Book.* Grand Rapids, Mich.: Phanes Press, 1997.

Conway, D.J. *Magickal Mystical Creatures.* Woodbury, Minn.: Llewellyn Publications, 2005.

Costello, Peter. *The Magic Zoo: the Natural History of Fabulous Animals.* New York: St. Martin's Press, 1979.

Dale-Green, Patricia. *Lore of the Dog.* Boston: Houghton Mifflin Co., 1967.

De Somer, Ruben. "Real Giants in the Low Countries?" *FATE Magazine,* January 2004.

"Devil." *Funk & Wagnall's New Encyclopedia.* Vol. 7. New York: Funk & Wagnall's Inc., 1979.

Ellis, Richard. *Monsters of the Sea.* Guilford, Conn.: Lyons Press, 2006.

Gaffron, Norma. *Unicorns: Great Mysteries, Opposing Viewpoints.* San Diego, Calif.: Greenhaven Press, 1989.

Gill, Sam D. and Irene F. Sullivan. *Dictionary of Native American Mythology.* New York: Oxford University Press, 1992.

Godfrey, Linda S. *The Beast of Bray Road: Tailing Wisconsin's Werewolf.* Madison, Wis.: Trails Books, 2003.

Godfrey, Linda S. *Hunting the American Werewolf.* Madison, Wis.: Trails Books, 2006.

Gould, Charles. *Mythical Monsters.* Whitefish, Mont.: Kessinger Publishing, 2003.

Guiley, Rosemary. *The Encyclopedia of Vampires, Werewolves, and Other Monsters.* New York: Checkmark Books, 2005.

Hamblin, Dora-Jane. *The First Cities.* New York: Time-Life Books, 1973.

Heuvelmans, Bernard (Chorvinsky, trans.). "Lingering Pterodactyls, Part One." *Strange Magazine,* no. 6 (1990).

Ions, Veronica. *Indian Mythology.* London, England: Drury House, 1967.

Jones, David M. and Brian L. Molyneaux. *Mythology of the American Nations.* London, England: Anness Publishing, 2006.

Joseph, Claudia. "Now Scientists Create a Sheep that's 15% Human," *Daily Mail.* Available online. URL: http://www.dailymail.co.uk/news/article-444436/Now-scientists-create-sheep-thats-15-human.html. Accessed on February 19, 2008.

Kruszelnicki, Karl S. "Mouse with Human Ear," ABC. Available online. URL: http://www.abc.net.au/science/k2/moments/s1644154.htm. Downloaded on May 9, 2008.

Kvideland, Reimund, and Henning K. Sehmsdorf, eds. *Scandinavian Folk Belief and Legend.* Minneapolis, Minn.: University of Minnesota, 1988.

Lake, Matt. *Weird Maryland, Your Travel Guide to Maryland's Local Legends and Best Kept Secrets.* New York: Sterling Publishing, 2006.

Land of the Devil. "Something Follows Campers in Sussex County," Land of the Devil Web site. Available online. URL: http://www.landofthedevil.com/Subtopics/Sigthings/sighting3.html. Posted on August 20, 2007.

Laytner, Ron. "The Mummy Makers," Edit International. Available online. URL: http://www.editinternational.com/read.php?id=47ddcf51d5a3e. Accessed on October 17, 2008.

Leeming, David Adams. "The Chimera." In *Mythical and Fabulous Creatures: A Sourcebook and Research Guide.* New York: Peter Bedrick Books, 1988.

Levins, Hoag. "Halloween Crossed with History," Historic Camden County. Available online. URL: http://historiccamdencounty.com/ccnews18.shtml. Posted on October 29, 2001.

Levy, Joel. *Fabulous Creatures and Other Magical Beings.* London, England: Carroll and Brown Publishers, Ltd., 2006.

Macklin, Karen. "Clone Home: Jellyfish DNA in a Rabbit? It's science; it's art; it's 'Gene(sis)' at the Berkeley Art Museum," *SF Weekly.* Available online. URL: http://www.ekac.org/sfweekly2003.html. Posted on September 3, 2003.

Marcum, Diana. "Leapin' Lizards! Valley couple's two-headed oddity of nature truly is one in a million—believe it or not." The Fresno Bee. Available online. URL: http://www.fresnobee.com/907/story/699961.html. Posted on June 29, 2008.

Markey, Sean. "Photo in the News: Two-Headed Turtle Found in China," National Geographic News. Available online. URL: http://news.nationalgeographic.com/news/2006/03/0317_060317_two_headed.html. Posted on September 3, 2008.

McHugh, Janie. "Legend of the Goatman still lives on in Bowie and around the world," The Bowie Blade-News. Available online. URL: http://www.hometownbowie.com/news/blade/2007/10/18-35. Posted on October 18, 2007.

Miles, Jim. "Pygmies and Giants." *FATE Magazine*, March 1985.

Mott, Maryann. "Animal-Human Hybrids Spark Controversy," National Geographic News. Available online. URL: http://news.nationalgeographic.com/news/pf/62295276.html. Posted on January 25, 2005.

The NIV Study Bible, Genesis 6:4. Grand Rapids, Mich.: Zondervan, 1985.

Petre, Jonathan. "Chimera embryos have right to life, say bishops," *Telegraph News.* Available online. URL: http://www.telegraph.co.uk/news/uknews/1555639/Chimera-embryos-have-right-to-life%2C-say-bishops.html. Posted on June 19, 2008.

Redford, Donald B., ed. *The Oxford Essential Guide to Egyptian Mythology.* New York: Berkley Books, 2003.

Rose, Carol. *Giants, Monsters and Dragons.* New York: W.W. Norton and Co., 2001.

Sceurman, Mark and Mark Moran. *Weird New Jersey: Your Travel Guide to New Jersey's Local Legends and Best Kept Secrets.* New York: Barnes & Noble, 2003.

Shuker, Karl P. N. "The Search for the Thunderbird Photo." *Strange Magazine*, no. 20, (December 1998).

Sorrow, Casey. "Patent attempted for human and ape lab chimeras," Monkeys in the News. Available online. URL: http://monkeydaynews.blogspot.com/2005/02/patent-attempted-for-human-and-ape-lab.html. Posted on February 14, 2005.

South, Malcolm, ed. *Mythical and Fabulous Creatures*. New York: Peter Bedrick Books, 1987.

Thompson, C.J.S. *The Mystery and Lore of Monsters*. New Hyde Park, N.Y.: University Books, 1968.

Further Resources

WEB SITES

American Folklore

http://www.americanfolklore.net/ee.html

A wide sampling of mythic creatures and stories from a variety of American cultures, including Native American, African American, Cajun, French Canadian, Scandinavian, and Spanish American.

Encyclopedia Mythica

http://www.pantheon.org

A vast, encyclopedic resource on mythology and folklore with images, definitions and stories from six geographical regions: Africa, Americas, Asia, Europe, Middle East, and Oceania.

Greek Mythology

http://www.greekmythology.com

Stories and lore on Greek gods, heroes, places, and fabulous creatures, with links to full-text online books such as *Bullfinch's Mythology* and volumes by ancient Greek and Roman authors Homer, Euripides, Sophocles, and others.

Land of the Devil

http://www.landofthedevil.com/Subtopics/Sightings/sighting3.html

A large Web site devoted to the lore of the legendary Jersey Devil, from the original history to new sightings and updates.

BOOKS

Arnold, Neil. *Monster! The A-Z of Zooform Phenomena*. North Devon, England: CFZ Press, 2007.

A dictionary-style compendium of cryptozoological or mystery animals and fabled creatures of legend from around the world, from the Romanian bogeyman called the Bau Bau to a beast called Sheepsquatch. The book is sparsely illustrated in black and white but very far ranging in subject matter.

Cotterell, Rachel and Arthur Storm. *The Ultimate Encyclopedia of Mythology*. London: Anness Publishing, 2006.

An oversized, coffee-table book featuring a comprehensive, lavishly illustrated cache of mythological lore from Eastern and Western ancient civilizations, enhanced by insightful sidebars.

Keel, John A. *The Complete Guide to Mysterious Beings*. New York: Tom Doherty Associates, 2002.

A probing inspection of contemporary mythic beings and cryptozoological creatures such as demon dogs, giants, Bigfoot, Man Birds, Mothman, and sea serpents by one of the most respected authorities on strange phenomena.

Levy, Joel. *Fabulous Creatures and Other Magical Beings*. London, England: Carroll and Brown Publishers, Ltd., 2006.

From chimeras to minotaurs, each creature is examined with historical art; photos of live, related animals; and a "fieldbook" report with zoological sketches and a list of main characteristics. This volume was produced in cooperation with the Cryptozoological Society of London.

Rose, Carol. *Giants, Monsters and Dragons*. New York: W.W. Norton and Co., 2001.

    A volume of cryptozoological, mythic, or symbolic creatures arranged alphabetically, with entries that describe each creature's appearance, history, and environment.

GAMES

Age of Mythology game series, Microsoft, 2002–2004

    Choose from a series of video editions or even a board game (2003) in this game that pits heroes against legendary monsters. Players may control armies from Greek, Egyptian, and Norse cultures, each with mythical creatures unique to its civilization.

God of War game series, Sony: *God of War* (2005), *God of War II* (2007), *God of War: Chains of Olympus* (2008), *God of War III* (2009)

    These Sony Playstation games are based on Greek mythology, starting with a single Spartan warrior fighting creatures such as Medusa, Cyclops, and the Hydra, and progressing to wars between the gods. In-game movies featuring the history of the Titans and other subjects enrich the understanding of the characters.

VIDEOS

Clash of the Titans (1981)
Metro-Goldwyn-Mayer, DVD

    Follow the adventures of the Greek hero Perseus as he tames Pegasus, captures Medusa, and battles the Kraken in this film.

Jason and the Argonauts (1963)
Columbia Pictures, DVD

The classic tale of Greek mythology featuring encounters with Harpies, the Talos, the Hydra, and other beasts as the heroes pursue the legendary Golden Fleece.

The Mothman Prophecies (2002)
Lakeshore Entertainment, DVD

Starring Richard Gere, this movie is a contemporary interpretation of a series of sightings of a humanoid, winged creature dubbed Mothman that occurred around the West Virginia town of Point Pleasant. The incidents were actually reported in the 1960s.

The Mummy (1932)
Universal, DVD

The eerie tale starring Boris Karloff that helped popularize the idea of Egyptian mummies as supernatural creatures.

Ulysses Against the Sons of Hercules (1961)
Compagnia Cinematografica Mondiale, DVD

Originally released in Italy, this film tells the story of the Greek heroes who must escape Cyclops, giant bird-men, and other legendary beings.

Vampire Secrets (2006)
History Channel, DVD

This review of vampires from different cultures digs back thousands of years, travels as far as Greece and China, and updates the concept of ancient human blood-drinkers with a look at Bram Stoker's fiendish Dracula and vampires rampant in today's pop culture.

Index

Italic page references indicate illustrations.

About the Author

LINDA S. GODFREY worked as a newspaper reporter and columnist for *The Week*, a county newspaper published in Delavan, Wisconsin, for 10 years. She won National Newspaper Association first-place awards for feature stories in 1996, 1998, and 2000. She is the author of *The Beast of Bray Road* and *Hunting the American Werewolf*, as well as two volumes in the Barnes & Noble "Weird" series: *Weird Wisconsin* (co-authored with Richard D. Hendricks), *Weird Michigan*, and *Strange Wisconsin*. She has appeared on many national television and radio programs as an expert on anomalous creatures, including *Inside Edition*, Animal Planet Channel, *The New In Search Of* (SCI FI Channel), Travel Channel, Discovery Kids, *Northern Mysteries* on Canada's Global Network, and the *Jeff Rense*, *Clyde Lewis*, *Rob McConnell*, and *Coast to Coast AM* radio shows. She is also an illustrator and artist, and she maintains a Web site on werewolf sightings and news at http://www.beastofbrayroad.com. She lives with her husband, Steven, in rural southeastern Wisconsin.

About the Consulting Editor

ROSEMARY ELLEN GUILEY is one of the foremost authorities on the paranormal. Psychic experiences in childhood led to her lifelong study and research of paranormal mysteries. A journalist by training, she has worked full time in the paranormal since 1983, as an author, presenter, and investigator. She has written 41 nonfiction books on paranormal topics, translated into 14 languages, and hundreds of articles. She has experienced many of the phenomena she has researched. She has appeared on numerous television, documentary, and radio shows. She is a columnist for *TAPS Paramagazine* and a consulting editor for *FATE* magazine. Ms. Guiley's books include *The Encyclopedia of Angels*, *The Encyclopedia of Magic and Alchemy*, *The Encyclopedia of Saints*, *The Encyclopedia of Vampires, Werewolves, and Other Monsters*, and *The Encyclopedia of Witches, Witchcraft and Wicca*, all from Facts On File. She lives in Connecticut and her Web site is http://www.visionaryliving.com.

A 2140 545742 4